Buying and Selling Coins

Other books by Michael Freeman

The Victorian Bronze Penny, 1860–1901
The Bronze Coinage of Great Britain

Michael Freeman

BUYING AND SELLING COINS

A Basic Guide

Barrie & Jenkins
London Melbourne Sydney Auckland Johannesburg

Barrie & Jenkins Ltd
An imprint of the Hutchinson Publishing Group
17–21 Conway Street, London W1P 6JD

Hutchinson Group (Australia) Pty Ltd
30–32 Cremorne Street, Richmond South, Victoria 3121
PO Box 151, Broadway, New South Wales 2007

Hutchinson Group (NZ) Ltd
32–34 View Road, PO Box 40-086, Glenfield, Auckland 10

Hutchinson Group (SA) (Pty) Ltd
PO Box 337, Bergvlei 2012, South Africa

First published 1983
© Michael Freeman 1983

Set in Monophoto Photina by Servis Filmsetting Ltd, Manchester
Printed in Great Britain by The Anchor Press
and bound by Wm Brendon & Son Ltd, both of Tiptree, Essex

ISBN 0 09 150401 5

Contents

Acknowledgements

I would like to express my thanks to Frank Purvey of Messrs B.A. Seaby Ltd for supplying many of the photographs used; to John Pearson Andrew, who writes regularly on coin investment in *The Daily Telegraph* and to Peter J. Seaby for supplying the statistics quoted; and to Messrs Seaby and *The Daily Telegraph* jointly for their permission to refer to the Seaby Index of Coin Prices.

Introduction

Coin collecting is an old-established hobby which has given, and continues to give, enjoyment to many thousands of people, world-wide. The study of coins – numismatics – has always been a serious and vital adjunct to historians and to those researching the social habits of Man. The 1970s saw the full emergence of a third reason for the acquisition of old coins – for investment or financial gain. Why?

During these years the Western world experienced a sustained period of inflation, which meant that in Britain, by the end of the decade, money purchased roughly one-quarter of what it did ten years earlier. Interest rates, while rising to abnormally high levels, were inadequate as protection of wealth and, with a prolonged world-wide trade recession making business and industrial investment generally seem uninviting, many people – and companies – looked to the world of antiques as a hedge against inflation. But why coins?

All antiques tend to rise in value because they are desired for their beauty, their historical importance, or their rarity. Translated into concrete terms, this means that a purchaser has to show the strength of his demand either by offering the prospective seller sufficient profit as inducement to sell or else by outbidding others for an item. In a free economy, where the laws of supply and demand operate, the rarity of an item – the limit of its availability – broadly determines its price. As all antiques are, by their nature, perpetually limited in their availability, the increasing demand for them results in rising prices. Paintings, furniture, silver and porcelain, with the disadvantages either of requiring care and expertise to preserve their condition, or of being bulky to house and obvious to thieves, or both, have proved highly satisfactory for many investors. Coins, however, needing only the slightest attention to preservation, have virtually none of the disadvantages and all the advantages of other antiques. As a group, coins proved at least as profitable as other forms of antiques investment in the late 1960s and 1970s.

They were, additionally, very undervalued, and may still be. The obvious comparison is with stamps. No coin of rarity and importance has yet fetched a price as high as a stamp of similar rarity and importance. Owing to the much larger number of stamp collectors, there has always been this disparity; but the gap is narrowing. In the 1960s particularly, coin prices rose dramatically from what are now obviously absurdly low figures, and in the 1970s the gap between them and those of stamps narrowed still further. Although there are rumours of a private sale in 1980 involving an Ancient Greek coin at US $1.5 million, the world's most valuable coin at the time of writing is a United States gold 'Brasher Doubloon' of 1787. It was auctioned for $725,000 late in 1979, while the most valuable stamp cost the buyer $935,000 in April 1980. As this indicates, the difference in value generally between top coins and top stamps is no longer marked. In fact, with a far longer history, there are many more valuable coins than stamps, and there is, therefore, much more money in coins as a whole.

It is both interesting and useful to compare coin prices of long ago with those of not-so-long ago and with those of today. In 1926 there was no market for a 1901 penny, even in extremely fine condition; in 1950 one could be bought for about 4p, and in 1982 for £1.75. But it is the dearer coins which show the most remarkable increases: a gold Angel of Henry VIII, not a rare coin, in very fine condition would have cost £1.12½ in 1926, £57.50 in 1966 and £350 in 1982. Really spectacular, both in percentage and real terms, has been the performance of very rare important coins such as a Henry VIII George-Noble, the first English coin to depict St George slaying the dragon, now and for over a hundred years the standard design on Britain's gold. In 1926 a very fine specimen would have cost about £30, by 1950 £135, but by 1982 could reasonably be expected to cost somewhere around £20,000! Many other remarkable comparisons can be made and will be found where relevant in later pages of this book.

In spite of such dramatic increases, the potential for further substantial appreciation looks good. A snowball effect is achieved by this belief, as investors are attracted by the profits to be made by steeply rising prices, which in turn are pushed upwards by investor demand.

This applies, of course, to other worthwhile investments; but one unique attribute which coins have, as near a guarantee of their eternal popularity as anything can be, is their significance as documentation of every period of every society that used them. Many other miscellaneous relics exist, but none affords the collector the opportunity to form a complete and continuous record of history better than coins. Indeed, they often provide the only true contemporary portraits of famous historical personages.

There is ample evidence of the increased interest in coins apart from the general rise in their price. The fact that the Royal Mint has found it a worthwhile enterprise to strike and package proof sets of British coins every year since 1970, as have the mints of many other countries, is indicative of this. Many countries also obtain income from striking and selling commemorative 'coins', most of them never intended for use as currency, but instead for sale to collectors. The Isle of Man, for example, has issued crowns, or 25p coins, almost every year since 1970, to commemorate such occasions as the Bicentenary of American Independence and the Centenary of the Horse-drawn Tram! A number of countries have struck special 'coins' depicting animals, part of the profits from which go towards helping the World Wildlife Conservation Fund.

Most of these 'modern commemoratives', as they are called, are of no interest to collectors of old coins. Some, indeed, would not call them coins at all, because they were not struck for the purpose of coins – to pass as currency. None the less, they have their devotees worldwide, because they are cheaper to buy than old coins in mint state and, of course, because they are attractive to look at; but only certain issues which are rare have increased in value to any worthwhile extent, while some have actually dropped below the introductory price. Probably the reason for this stems basically from the fact that they appeal mainly to the casual collector rather than to the serious, and initial interest wanes more quickly when one is only casually interested. There is no shortage of many modern commemoratives, as their owners decide to sell much more readily than do those who have devoted long years of patient study and endeavour in order to acquire a collection of old coins. Many collectors of old coins form an attachment to them with less of an eye on market trends, and the most worthwhile collections, containing coins which are difficult to obtain, may be the result of a lifetime of collecting.

By far the largest proportion of coin trading is in issues which were once used as currency, and, as the history of coinage started over 2,600 years ago, there are very many different types. The man-in-the-street has little knowledge of coins which he has not actually used as currency, but tends to be intrigued mainly by their antiquity and value. Most homes have a few, usually low-value, coins in a box or drawer, and news headlines which mention coins worth thousands of pounds kindle hopes of a quick and easy fortune. This applies particularly to recent coins, such as a 1933 or 1954 penny of Great Britain. Only eight of the former are known, and the latter is unique, reportedly exchanging hands in 1980 for £30,000. Most people can understand that a large and impressive gold or silver coin struck centuries ago has a high value, but a modern copper just like the ones they used to spend . . . ?

To the majority of serious coin collectors, modern coins offer little of interest, lacking any historical significance and, for the most part, stereotyped in design. Most collectors specialise – that is, restrict what they collect, perhaps to coins of a particular country, period of time, or of a certain denomination. There are numerous possibilities – almost as many as there are types of coins. Advice usually received on the matter of investment comes from dealers who recommend the purchase of *any* coin, or any type of coin, which appeals to the collector, in as good condition as he can afford. Certainly, any collectable coin will, over a period, rise in value, purely in response to rising expenses and the willingness of collectors to accept price rises as inevitable; but, in reality, the majority of coins are not satisfactory as investments. The word 'junk' is relative. It is also an emotive word, but the sad truth is that very little demand exists for most coins in the lower grades of preservation. Almost always, to sell them a dealer will need to offer the inducement of a low price, and even then, most will agree, it is a lot easier to sell a choice coin at a normal price. To buy them, a dealer will need a similar inducement, and it is this fact which most collectors fail to appreciate until they try to sell them. It would be more helpful for dealers to advise collectors seeking advice on investment and who cannot afford to buy and hold a collection of top-quality coins, to collect purely for their enjoyment and not to entertain high hopes of a profit. Between, roughly, 1960 and 1970, coin prices 'took off' and handsome profits were and are available for anyone who bought anything at all before then. The dealers' advice was proved correct. In the 1970s, however, under the increasing influence of investor demand for 'the best', the price of 'junk' has fallen further and further away. Even in the long term now, the prices of lower-grade coins seldom come near to keeping pace with inflation.

It has always been valid to advise investment in quality: now it is imperative. Statistics seem to show average common coins rising in value, modestly, almost keeping pace with more choice rare coins in some instances. These statistics refer to *selling* price: there is none which shows what is being *paid* for ordinary coins. If there were any, they would show an increasing profit margin on such coins, made necessary, if a dealer is to find it worth his while handling them at all, by his ever-increasing expenses in a period of high inflation.

For this reason, it must be borne in mind, any prices referred to in the pages that follow are included merely for comparison and to indicate the extent and direction of price movement: they are *not* values.

The headlines one reads refer only to record high prices being paid in auction – lack of success is less newsworthy and is thus not publicised. It is very easy to get the wrong impression of coin values from reading auction reports and catalogues. By reading the following chapters the reader will, I hope, achieve a balanced picture of the market for coins and be able to separate those factors which are relevant from those which are not, in the search for profitable transactions.

Nor are accurate and meaningful statistics proof of anything except past results. Although they may be helpful in forecasting future trends, when considered along with other available information, they promise nothing. *Inflation Shelters*, published by the Economist Intelligence Unit, puts it thus: 'The worst possible reason for buying an object is to be seduced by the belief that prices will continue to rise inexorably and that profits are inevitable.' Nothing is guaranteed.

The best approach is to understand why some coins appreciate in value while others do not; to make reasonable assumptions for the future, based on knowledge of the relevant factors; and to know how and when to buy and to sell, most effectively. I have adopted this as my framework in the chapters which follow.

1

How to identify coins correctly

It might appear obvious that accurate identification is essential to anyone financially involved with coins, yet, as every dealer knows, errors and inaccuracies in classifying and grading condition are probably the single factor which contributes most to his success in being able to buy cheaply. It is one thing to know you have, say, a penny of Henry I, and another thing entirely to know enough to be able to say which type it is – there are fifteen major types – how to grade its condition, allowing for the imperfections in striking frequently encountered in coins of this period, and thereby correctly to determine its value. A poorly struck or badly worn specimen of the most common type would be worth about £50, while a superb specimen of the rarest type might fetch £4,000. 'Correct identification' therefore means 'complete identification'.

If you take your coins to a dealer for identification, there is more than a chance that you will be informed fully only if they are worth little. The truth is that a dealer's coins are only part of his stock-in-trade: the other part is his knowledge and expertise. There is no such thing as 'fixed prices' in coins – all prices are, within certain limitations, negotiable. A dealer can trade only by buying for less than he can sell for, and the margin of his success is measured by the difference. Few dealers would actually lie when asked to identify coins of substantial value; but there are different levels of identification. Most would give the reign and denomination of a coin; very, very few would draw attention to a rare date or variety or, the most important

Silver pennies of Henry I (1100–35)
(see page 21 for an explanation of grading terms)

Type 15, VF, £140 (1978)   Type 13, GF, £475 (1979)

Type 5, EF, struck at
Cambridge and therefore
unique. Valued at about
£4,000

Medieval coins are often difficult to classify without the use of catalogues,
but differences in values show the importance of correct classification

---

determinant of value, to a coin being in exceptionally good condition.
The most honest valuation, and one which cannot be criticised in any
way, will be given as 'what your coins are worth to me' – i.e. he may
make an offer for them. What they could be worth to *you* if you sell
elsewhere may be another matter entirely, so in general do not rely
too heavily on the stated comments of those with a vested interest in
what you know or do not know. Before committing yourself to buying
or selling, it is important to know exactly what you have or hope to
buy, whether or not it is a rare variety, and its correct grading of
condition. Only then can the value be determined.

By making it clear that you want a written valuation and are not
interested in selling the coins, you should obtain what you want from
an honest and knowledgeable dealer. As an expert, he will make a
charge for his services – perhaps 1–2 per cent of the value – as he is
entitled to do. In general, valuations thus made tend to be on the low
side, particularly at times when prices are rising, as, if necessary, the
valuer may be required to justify them, perhaps to settle an insurance
claim. He would do this by taking his figures from a standard,
generally accepted, catalogue of coin values. These tend to be worked
out some time before the book is published, when prices may have

changed to a significant extent, and also often give values only for general types, ignoring the effect on value of rare varieties.

While it cannot be to his benefit to reveal the full potential of a coin he may hope to buy, the rôle of the coin dealer is not primarily to profit from the ignorance of the seller. It is only fair, in mitigation, to point out that, as well as having to make his living or maximise his profits from his superior knowledge, he also achieves this from gaining the confidence and good-will of his customers and the establishment of a reputation for fair dealing, from which results increased volume of trade. He provides a service to collectors by being an accessible market for both buyers and sellers. He may help to locate specific coins required by collectors, knowing where or how to look for them. Some dealers promote the study of numismatics by publishing articles giving information on various academic levels, along with their lists of coins for sale. Often coins have to be held by them for a long time before they are sold, so the eventual profit must hopefully compensate the dealer for interest he would have received on his money if he had not used it to buy and hold coins. To deal successfully, he will have to invest in a large library of reference books which he can consult, and subscribe to auctioneers' and other dealers' lists, in order to keep abreast of the latest movements in prices. This outlay must be paid for and justify itself from profits. Finally, even the most experienced dealer

---

A very old coin, generally, will be impossible for someone without experience to identify in any way. It is then necessary to seek help so that, at least, the correct catalogue may be used to pin-point it more precisely. Some forms of currency are in fact so strange that only experts can identify them as such

Irish gold 'ring' money, about 200 BC, £2,000 (1978)

Russian spiral copper currency, possibly fourteenth–sixteenth century, £90 (1979)

can make factual mistakes and errors of judgement. Unless he is certain, it is only sensible for him to err on the side of safety by not risking the possibility of overpaying.

If you know only which country your coin is from, and its date, it should still not be too difficult to find out the rest. When asked, an obliging dealer will take the trouble to show you the catalogue reference to it in the book he uses to identify coins of that country or of that particular type. A museum or large library can also supply the book you want, and museums can often be more helpful than any other source of information. They will not, however, venture into the realm of valuations, and further checking for these will be necessary after identification.

  Tin money from Kent, 50 BC–AD 50, a crude copy of Greek or Roman coins, with the head of Apollo on the obverse and a bull on the reverse, VF, £75 (1976), less by 1982

Early Anglo-Saxon silver sceat, AD 600–775, nearly EF, £200 (1977)

Silver penny of Eadred (946–55), nearly EF, £225 (1977)

Most coins before about 1600 do not carry a date, and the style of lettering on early coins is often very unlike that on modern pieces, making it difficult for many people to know even where to start. If it is at all possible to make an assumption regarding where the coin originated, by looking through the photographs in a catalogue for that country, you should be able to find coins which look the same or similar. If so, by reading the descriptions and comparing them carefully with the details of your coin, you should be able to make a precise identification. Unfortunately, the tendency for really old coins to be worn or mis-struck can mean that important areas are indecipherable. Even so, an expert can make at least a general, and

Silver groat (fourpence), Henry VII (1485–1509), last issue of a type struck for over two hundred years, with minor variations distinguishing one reign from another, GVF, £85 (1979)

sometimes even a precise, classification with only a little of the detail visible.

For the identification of most coins less than two hundred years old, you should have little difficulty if you consult *The Standard Catalog of World Coins*, compiled from information supplied by hundreds of experts.* Published anew each year, this is a massive, but clearly arranged, listing of every coin issued by every country since the late eighteenth century; and it includes all kinds of identification aids, numerous photographs, and valuations for each coin in various grades. Assistance in deciphering unfamiliar alphabets is given as well. If required to be used fairly often, it should more than repay its price, which in 1982 was about £20. Although no substitute for a good specialist book and sometimes more than a little way out for prices not carefully adjusted from previous editions, it is a most useful guide and is crammed full of information. Most coin dealers also sell catalogues and will gladly advise on which to buy or consult for particular coins.

One pitfall for the inexperienced is that they think a coin with a countermark – usually a small design or number stamped into the surface – loses value. From the earliest days of coin issue, in Europe about 700 BC, both individuals and governments have occasionally marked coins by counterstamping or mutilation, in order to use them for a purpose other than that intended by the issuing state. Normally any mark inflicted by an individual detracts from the value as it has no significance. On the other hand, an official countermark will often add to the value because it changes the identity of the coin and because marked coins are always decidedly rarer than unmarked ones.

Some of the most commonly counterstruck coins are the Spanish-American silver eight reales pieces, struck in quantity in various South American towns and hijacked for use as currency by many

---

*Compiled by Krause and Mishler and published by Krause Publications, Iola, Wisconsin, USA.

Aspendus, Ancient Greece, third–fourth century BC silver stater. The significance of counter-marks on this, and on other ancient coins, is uncertain, and they have no effect on value, VF. £150 (1979)

Caribbean island of Tortola, half- dollar, 1805–24, made from a cut segment of a Mexican dollar, countermarked; coin F, countermark GVF, £60 (1978)

Great Britain, a Mexican dollar (or eight reales), countermarked with the bust of George III and issued at a value of four shillings and nine pence, GVF, £150 (1979)

Berne, Switzerland, forty batzen, countermarked on a French silver écu; coin GF, countermark GVF, £125 (1980)

countries which were short of silver. This occurred most frequently during the period 1760–1810. In Britain the coins were stamped with a small effigy of George III and issued as legal tender to a value of four shillings and nine pence, slightly below the value of a crown which was five shillings. One of these coins is shown here, as is a silver

French écu with countermarks on both sides denoting the coin's use by the city of Berne, prior to the establishment of a Swiss state, at a value of forty batzen. Countermarked coins are listed in catalogues under the heading of the reissuing state or country. In view of the possibility that a countermark may make a coin valuable, it is advisable, if you do not know its significance, to ask someone who does. No catalogue of South American or French coins will correctly identify these two coins, but instead, reference to them should be found in books on British and Swiss coins respectively, and their values discovered to be increased by five or six times from £30 and £20 by the addition of the countermarks.

The significance of the two countermarks on the Ancient Greek silver stater also shown opposite is unfortunately lost in the mists of time. Such coins, from Aspendus in Pamphylia, occur with various different marks, probably to make them current officially in other cities and states, as in more recent times. The presence or otherwise of countermarks on ancient coins generally has no effect on their value. This stater dates from 385–370 BC, and has a value of around £150.

Errors represent another area where the novice can go far astray in estimating their effect on value, this time by being over-optimistic. Coin production today is by means of precisely operated machinery, resulting in virtually identical coins by the million. Apart from Ancient Greece and Rome, the further back one goes in time, the more primitive were the tools of the coiner. So many dies were used that little importance is attached to minor deviations in inscription and design until the mid-seventeenth century, when the coin 'mill' permanently replaced striking by hand. As might therefore be expected, most errors prior to the introduction of machinery, being far more common, usually have little, if any, extra value; while the more recent the coin with a rare and important error, the greater is the factor by which its value is enhanced. Examples illustrated overleaf show a third of a farthing, struck for use in Malta, with the letter 'G' of 'REG' completely absent, and also a British sixpence of 1878 with the 'B' of 'BRITANNIAR' overstruck, by mistake, with a 'D'. The little copper coin is a 'proof', that is, a rare trial coin struck from polished dies, and in virtually the same condition as when new, so in 1978 it was worth £350 instead of £40, which an ordinary coin in mint state without the error would have been worth. The error sixpence, also in the highest state of preservation, was sold for £150 in January 1976,

Proof third-farthing, Victoria, 1844, with error 'RE' instead of 'REG', about UNC., with slight scratch, £350 (1978)

Sixpence, Victoria, 1878, with error 'DRITANNIAR' instead of 'BRITANNIAR', about UNC., £150 (1976), but worth substantially more by 1982

when the normal coin of this date fetched only £20. It pays to have a keen eye! By contrast, medieval coins with letters missing are so common that not only do they fetch the same price as normal coins, but dealers and auctioneers often do not bother even to mention such peculiarities.

2
How to grade coins correctly

Once you know which types of coin you have, and before you can hazard a guess at their value, it is essential to know how good is their state of preservation, or 'grading'. There are standard terms used throughout the Western world, and although the terminology may differ from one language to another, each grade has its equivalent. In Britain the accepted grades run down from UNCIRCULATED, EXTREMELY FINE, VERY FINE, FINE, FAIR, to POOR. As a guide, overleaf are examples of the top five grades on five coins of a similar type – the last two are patterns and were not intended to circulate, but did!

UNCIRCULATED (UNC.): As issued. No wear; possibly very minor imperfections.
EXTREMELY FINE (EF): Sharp details; very slight signs of circulation.
VERY FINE (VF): Slight flattening on high areas due to a little wear.
FINE (F): Considerable flattening; details very faint.
FAIR: Details of design worn away; main features and inscriptions still distinguishable.

UNC. copper and bronze coins will usually, but not always, have their original golden or reddish 'mint lustre', and greater value attaches to coins with this. In time, from exposure to the atmosphere, it dulls to the normal brown colour. EF copper and bronze will have, at

Uncirculated   Extremely fine

Very fine   Fine

Examples of the top five grades on
five coins of a similar type

Fair

best, only traces of lustre, as the dulling process occurs, and is
accelerated, during circulation.

Occasionally a coin may be graded as any of the above, but with a
qualification, such as 'EF for issue'. This means that coins of this issue,
or type, were all badly struck, and this particular one is in a better

state of preservation than its appearance might indicate. Examples are usually to be found amongst coins of the Middle Ages and may include, in extreme cases, specimens without wear but with flat areas. To an inexperienced eye, a flat area would seem to disqualify any coin from the higher grades and thus result in it being undervalued. Only by reading or by examining such coins will you get to know which types were weakly or badly struck and make allowances accordingly when grading them. Correspondingly, a well-struck specimen of a type normally badly struck will be an exception and be worth more.

Testoon (shilling), Henry VIII (1509–47), nearly VF, £480 (1977). This type was normally poorly struck so the flattened areas are not the result of wear, and it must be graded higher than its appearance indicates

Shilling (obverse), Philip and Mary (1554–8), another issue which was usually poorly struck, F – for this issue

Sixpence, Edward VI (1547–53), nearly EF and rarely found in such good condition, £225 (1976). (Comparable values: VF £65, F £25)

Farthing, James II, 1687, tin, with *official* copper plug, as normal, nearly VF, £200 (1976). An inexperienced person might assume, wrongly, a low value due to damage

Although it must be stressed that photographs may not show the surface details or colour, they are undoubtedly useful as a second-best to examining actual coins in enabling one to learn the standards applying in grading. Subscribing to one of the larger dealers' coin lists will result in the building up of a good collection of coin photographs of all types, with the grades assessed by an expert, and this will be an authoritative source for forming one's own judgements on grading.

It is best, of course, to examine as many coins as possible. Normally only a dealer or museum expert will have the opportunity to handle a large number; but experience can be acquired both by viewing an auction held by a firm known for its expertise and by looking at coins offered for sale by a dealer with a reputation for fair grading.

Sometimes the condition of one side of a coin may be better than that of the other. Abbreviations are normally used, so such a coin might be described thus: VF/EF. The first grade mentioned, VERY FINE, is that of the obverse – the side with the head or name of the ruler – and the second, EXTREMELY FINE, that of the reverse or 'tails' side.

A further refinement is used to describe a coin which falls slightly short of, or is slightly better than, one of the established grades. One might thus find NF (nearly FINE) or GF (good FINE), NVF, GVF, and so on.

As even slight differences in grading represent differences in value, it is important to be as accurate as one can be when buying, not necessarily accepting the grading of the owner, who may try to exaggerate the quality of his coins. Even slight overgrading really matters with coins in or near mint state, or UNC. as this is usually described. There is not that much difference at a casual glance between a coin in UNC. condition and one in EF or GEF; but the value of a truly choice coin may be double or more that of an EF one. In actual terms, this can be a large amount of money. It will certainly matter a lot more than will overgrading at the other end of the scale; and more for a valuable coin than a cheap one.

This point is made clear in any catalogue which gives values. The examples on page 25 are from the 1982 Seaby Index, which is published periodically by *The Daily Telegraph*:

Generally, the older the coin the rarer it is in EF and UNC.; hence the omissions for the three oldest gold coins, the sale of which in these grades seldom occurs. When it does, there may be quite astonishing

	F	VF	EF	UNC.
WILLIAM III, Crown, 1696, 1st bust	£30	£120	£600	
GEORGE III, Shilling, 1787	4	10	25	
GEORGE IV, Shilling, 1821		18	65	£120
VICTORIA, Crown, 1845		50	500	1,250
EDWARD VII, Half-crown, 1902		14	50	80
EDWARD III, gold 'Treaty' Noble (undated) (London mint)	300	600		
HENRY VII, Sovereign (undated)	7,500	17,500		
ELIZABETH I, Pound (undated) (Mintmark 'O')	1,000	2,750		
ANNE, Guinea, 1714	150	375	1,250	
GEORGE V, Half-sovereign, 1912		40	55	

results, as witnessed in auction in June 1980, when an Elizabeth I gold ryal, catalogued at £4,750 in VF condition, realised £22,000. That specimen was graded EF, well-struck, and toned.

At the top end of the grading scale, when minor imperfections can mean major differences in value, it is surprising that other countries have not followed the example of the United States, where the grade 'UNCIRCULATED' is subdivided into a numerical category which indicates quality of strike as well as condition. An absolutely flawless coin, if such exists, would be 'MS (Mint State) 70' and the lowest collectable grade perhaps 'AG (Almost Good) 3'. The lowest number for an UNC. specimen is MS-60, which would indicate light surface marks or a weak striking. Various numbers between 60 and 70 are used to denote the subtle shades of imperfection; and just how much this matters to the value is vividly brought home by the following extract from the September 1981 sales list of a leading US dealer.

	MS-60	MS-63	MS-65
Trade $1 1877	$795	$1,795	$3,995
5c, 1883 (no 'CENTS')	$65	$125	$495
1c, 1857–8	$395	$695	$1,795

Certain coins are very seldom found in MS-65 or better, perhaps owing to poor-quality striking or damage to the dies, and there is then an enormous difference in value between the highest grades and anything less. As might be expected, the older the coin the less likely one is to obtain a top-grade specimen, although, as will be explained, this is not always the case.

For comparison, here is a table listing the equivalent British and American grades:

UK	USA
FDC (Fleur de Coin)	Proof 60–70 (Used only for proofs – special trial strikings)
UNC. (Uncirculated)	MS (Mint State) 60–70
EF (Extremely Fine)	⎰ AU (Almost Uncirculated) 50–59
	⎱ XF (Extremely Fine) 40–49
	(31–39 not normally used)
VF (Very Fine)	VF (Very Fine) 20–30
F (Fine)	F (Fine) 10–19
Fair	⎰ VG (Very Good) ⎱ 5–9
	⎱ G (Good)
Mediocre *or* Poor	AG (Almost Good) 1–4

In America the ANA (American Numismatic Association)* has tried to establish uniform standards of grading, in order to eliminate the chaos which results from subjective judgements on the condition of a coin. It produces a useful booklet as a guide to the standard grades, and will issue certificates giving the grade of coins submitted to the Association for this purpose. In time, no doubt, objective grading will be universal. Until then, it is important to learn from knowledgeable and reputable sources, and to remember that seductive descriptions like 'gem' and 'choice' are pure sales patter, and have no place in objective numismatic terminology.

The grade applied to a coin indicates only the degree of wear – loss of material – normally fairly evenly distributed on both sides. To be correct, the description of a coin will also mention any other features which affect the appearance, the desirability, and hence the value. A commonly encountered defect is an edge knock – 'EK', as it is

---

*The address is given on page 90.

abbreviated in some dealers' lists – and this will affect value, only to a slight extent on a low-grade coin, which has other unattractive features, but increasingly the higher the grade. A coin otherwise in mint state may lose a third of its value if the dent on the edge is very noticeable.

When edge knocks occur, it is usually on the thicker coins of the last three hundred years or so. Most coins from about AD 600 to 1600 were thin and suffered other forms of defacement. The thinness of the metal often resulted in cracks occurring and also allowed the coins to be bent easily. Even when straightened again, such coins show a 'crease' along the line of the bend. Thin gold and silver coins were easy to 'clip', i.e. metal was illegally trimmed off the edge. Because they were struck by hand, the tools used were applied with less precision or care than on later, machine-made, coins. Sometimes the dies bearing the designs were not correctly lined up with the centre of the blank piece of metal or, if the blank was not evenly flat, certain portions of the design would be less clearly impressed on to it than would others.

So, even if a coin has suffered no wear, these and other forms of defacement, such as scratches, corrosion and cleaning, all have a significant effect on value and must be included in any correct description of its condition. The effect of a really obvious imperfection, on average, is to lower the value by about a full grade from that which it would have been without the imperfection. Of course, each flaw or defect must be judged individually. One which, say, obliterates the date or spoils the appearance of the monarch's face will have a greater impact on the value of the coin than one which impairs an area of lesser importance.

Needless to say, absolutely perfect coins are many times rarer than imperfect ones. Most have suffered from some degree of mishandling which could have been avoided. Care must be taken not to drop a coin, obviously, but many non-collectors are unaware that no coin should ever be polished to make it 'like new again'. If there has been any wear at all, no amount of polishing will restore the sharpness of detail. On the contrary, it will further flatten the high points slightly and, even if only visible under a magnifying glass, an indispensable accessory for detecting defects, leave light scratches which un-questionably lower the desirability of a coin. The artificial brilliance of a polished coin is obvious to most people who have any experience with coins, and the same applies to a copper coin which has been dipped or polished in order to restore the golden or reddish 'mint lustre' it had when issued. The genuine lustre of a new copper coin has not been successfully reproduced by artificial means.

Always hold a coin by the edge and never on the surface. Even if you do not leave an immediately visible fingerprint, the slight amount of acid thus deposited will react with the metal over a period of time, and will show up some day. Any organic matter, such as dandruff and even a sneeze or cough, should not be allowed to touch a coin. The better the condition of the coin, the greater will be the effect on its value of an unsightly spot of corrosion or discoloration. This is most important in connection with proofs – trial coins not intended for circulation and struck with care from, usually, polished dies. These have a mirror-like 'field' – background to the design – with contrasting frosted designs, and, as a result, they are more attractive than normal currency issues. When a proof is impaired, the field has usually been scuffed and the effect is lessened, sometimes to the extent that it is almost indistinguishable from a currency coin.

Any coin which has a mount is, to a coin dealer or collector, reduced virtually to the level of bullion or an item of jewellery, and has

Proof shilling, 1956, mint state, £100 (1976)

Proof five pounds, 1839, with the famous and beautiful 'Una and the Lion' reverse, nearly FDC, £8,250 (1978)

value only as such, unless of considerable rarity. Even the trace of a mount is sufficient to have a substantial effect on value. The presence of a hole or a 'plug' – a filled-in hole – even if well-camouflaged, is exactly comparable to the effect of a mount or trace of a mount, respectively.

Through ignorance, it is easy to underestimate the value of a coin. Equally, with inadequate knowledge and wishful thinking, it is easy to deceive oneself into thinking one's coins have higher grades, and are therefore more valuable than they really are. Objectivity is vital when your finances depend upon your judgement! Normally you can rely on the opinions of the larger and better-known dealers and auctioneers, who maintain strictly the standards which apply to grading. When they do err, it is on the side of safety, by undergrading, in order to establish confidence among their customers who will then buy or bid for coins unseen, in the knowledge that they will be at least as good as described, if not better. Unfortunately there are others who grossly overstate the grading of their coins to prey on the ignorant, so it is undoubtedly important, in assessing the value of a coin, to be sure of its correct grading.

If a coin is valuable, it may have been worth someone's time and effort to make it appear so. Always use a magnifying glass to look out

for traces of evidence that it has, in some way, been touched up. The obvious alteration to beware of is one to the date – there are more 1933 pennies which started life as 1935 than there are genuine ones, for example. Rather less fraudulent but still a form of deception are 'improvements', such as filing off a mount and re-engraving milling on the edge. As this never results in exactly identical notches, it pays to examine the edge carefully for this, for any variation in colour of metal, which might indicate plugging, or for any other suspicious-looking irregularity.

3

How to take care of your coins

Having become aware of the importance of condition, you will want to know what steps to take to prevent deterioration or, if possible, to improve the appearance of your coins.

As usual, prevention is far better and easier than cure. The 'don'ts' have already been explained – don't drop, don't polish, and don't finger the surface. If you disobey, it is impossible to restore a coin successfully to its previous condition. The only improvement usually possible is the removal of dirt, and this requires care. Gold and silver may be cleaned by gentle washing in warm, soapy water. Avoid salt water, which will corrode. Drying must be by absorption, as light rubbing with material, no matter how soft, may leave faint scratches. Cotton-wool can be recommended to soak up droplets.

Copper or bronze coins should never be washed, and must always be kept dry. Even a damp atmosphere will have a disastrous effect, resulting in verdigris, a green corrosive substance. A dealer or a museum expert should be consulted if you wish to remove verdigris from a coin, as, although any damage already done cannot entirely be rectified, it is possible to stop it from spreading. To remove dirt from copper and bronze coins, very soft non-nylon brushes are best. Lead and tin coins which have started to corrode are similarly best left to experts.

It is very important not to confuse undesirable foreign matter on the surface of a coin with the prized benefit known as 'toning'. This is a natural darkening or colouring which comes with prolonged exposure of metal to certain non-destructive chemicals in the atmosphere. If it has formed evenly, this will enhance the value of a coin. Silver is particularly receptive, turning blackish or, more desirably, an attractive blue, green or golden colour, depending on the particular chemicals to which it was exposed. No attempt should be made to remove it or to create it artificially, as any unnatural appearance or suggestion that a coin has been tampered with in any way will detract quite substantially from its desirability. This applies particularly to the original lustre on copper or bronze coins, the presence of which adds to their value. Once it has disappeared, it cannot be restored, and any attempt to do so will, to any experienced numismatist, be obvious.

The best method of preserving condition is by careful storage. Albums with plastic pages divided into many small 'pouches' may retain moisture and are less suitable for copper or bronze than for coins in other metals; and care has to be taken that coins do not fall out. Although much more expensive, mahogany cabinets with doors and felt-lined cut-outs are the choice of museums and dealers. Cabinets made of oak are not to be recommended because of the fumes released by that wood, which can attack the surface of some coins. An additional protection is to wrap coins in specially treated soft tissue paper; this will prevent minute particles from landing on them and isolate the metal from possibly harmful chemicals in the atmosphere.

Having read the above, you can now be expected to have identified your coins, have established their condition, know how to store them, and have worked out their book value. If you have consulted the right books but not been able to find in them a coin you have, you may have an unknown coin – unlikely, but always possible – or a 'pattern', which is a trial piece of a type not adopted for currency, usually very rare and thus valuable; or else a forgery.

It does not automatically follow that discovery of an unknown coin means it is worth an enormous amount. Very many designs and variations of design occur on ancient coins, and most discoveries that are made of 'unknown' coins are of those struck between 1,500 and 2,500 years ago. If it is a relatively minor variation from the normal, whether ancient or modern, there will probably be few buyers keen enough to pay much more specially for it; and even if it is a major discovery, if it is in poor condition or belongs to a general type which is of low value, the increased value attached to it will not be of great proportions. Because it is discovered to be unique, what would have

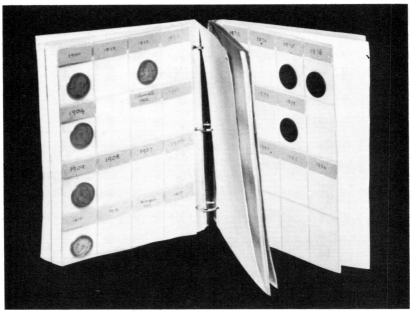

Coin album (top) and Coin cabinet

The fact that some, very rare, halfpennies of 1862 have a small letter – A, B or C – to the left of the lighthouse was not discovered until 1970; nearly EF, £135 (1975), but without the letter, the coin would have been worth only about £7

been a £1 coin may become a £10 one, whereas a £100 coin may become a £1,000 coin, or more. There is an important exception. The collecting of modern coins is always by date, so the best discovery to make is likely to prove to be an unknown date in a popular modern series, such as the 1952 British half-crown. The only one known was discovered in circulation and sold for £2,000 in 1969. Its current value is unknown but certain to be many times more. Needless to say, half-crowns of other years of this period have very little value, if any, even in mint state: it is the date 1952 which makes the difference.

Another possibility, when you cannot find reference to a coin in the correct catalogue, is that it may be a pattern, with either one or both sides different in some way from the current coin of that date. The example used to illustrate the grading 'Fine' on page 22 is a pattern penny which was struck in 1862, 1865 and 1870. The reverse is identical to that of the currency penny, but the obverse shows Queen Victoria wearing a coronet, instead of a garland of leaves. Also illustrated here is a pattern penny of 1895 with the obverse as adopted

Pattern penny, Victoria, 1895, only about five known, about mint state, £650 (1975)

for currency but, on the reverse, a dotted cross and border above and around Britannia. These were omitted from the approved reverse. Although they occasionally passed into circulation by mistake, patterns are normally found in mint state or near it. While some countries, at certain periods, seemed to produce a relatively high number of patterns, most are of great rarity, and because of this and the fact that they are not part of the regular series of currency coins, they are seldom included in the more popular catalogues. A specialist book, on the other hand, will be as thorough as possible on its particular subject and should include all patterns relating to the coins covered.

Few British patterns were struck in quantity, but two which were are the 'model' penny and halfpenny with a copper outer ring and an inner section, usually of a tin alloy but sometimes also of copper. These little 'coins' were struck in Birmingham in 1844 privately by

(Enlarged) 'model' penny, struck in 1844 privately,
very common, worth only £1 or £2 in EF

Joseph Moore, an engineer, who hoped to receive a government contract, as others had previously, to make coins for Britain and her overseas possessions. In order to prove that they would be acceptable as alternatives to the much larger and heavier copper ones already in circulation, he himself 'issued' thousands of his 'coins'; and the fact that many are found with wear is proof that they were accepted by the public although not legal tender. Today most types can be bought for as little as £1 or £2.

Forgeries fall basically into two categories: those contemporary with the coin forged and intended to pass as currency, and later forgeries, usually of a valuable rare coin, intended to deceive collectors. Normally forgeries made before about 1800 are easy to detect, being crude attempts to imitate with the use of unsophisticated equipment and usually in a cheaper metal coated to resemble gold or silver, or else of short weight. Modern forgeries tend to be more difficult to detect and pass unnoticed by all except experts. Their occurrence is, unfortunately, sufficiently frequent to have justified the setting up of the International Association for the Suppression of Counterfeit Coins.* Various Western countries either have a branch or their own equivalent, and museums and dealers will readily refer to this non-profit-making concern if the authenticity of a coin is in question. If the Association confirms a coin to be a forgery, it may confiscate the coin or mark it in such a way that it cannot again be sold as, or thought to be, genuine. In some numismatic magazines, publicity is given to newly discovered forgeries, in case further specimens of the same type turn up. It can be worthwhile to subscribe to such publications and, if in doubt, to show a suspect coin to an expert.

Certain Greek and Roman coins which are of superb design and workmanship have attracted the attention of imitators over the centuries, and there are many counterfeits of, particularly, large Greek silver and large Roman copper coins. It is sometimes possible to distinguish a fake ancient coin by its 'soapy' feel or slightly blurred details, or else by a split *around* the edge. Museum experts are always interested to see Greek and Roman coins, and some even have a collection of forgeries with which to compare, for reference, to enable them to confirm if a coin shown to them is genuine or not. Some will supply a certificate of authenticity, which can be useful in establishing confidence when selling.

---

* The telephone number is given on page 90.

4

How to value coins correctly

Most collectors wrongly believe they need only to identify a coin, assess its grade, and look it up in the most recent catalogue, in order to value it correctly. While 'book values' may be useful as a guide, they can seldom be more, and may even, on occasion, be misleading.

Almost all priced catalogues are written by dealers who state that 'values' are based on their selling prices, and not what they will pay. No one reading their books can therefore expect anything like 'catalogue' prices from dealers for their coins, so, as most coins are bought by the trade, they are not, to the seller, worth their 'book value'.

Even if the book is new, the values stated in it will have been worked out at least some months before it went to print, thus, in the case of coins which have since gained or lost popularity, rendering their values out-of-date. Many of the rarer coins in the book will not have appeared on the market for years, so guesses have to be made or the value omitted altogether. This also applies to pre-nineteenth-century coins in the top grade which seem to fluctuate in value on every occasion they are sold.

As this implies, it is as important to know the strength of demand as it is to know a 'book value'. The best method of discovering this, short of actually selling, is to make a careful comparison of dealers' lists and auction prices realised, at different periods of time. A static price indicates low demand, which in turn means the 'value' has dropped;

whereas a substantial jump in price can confidently be interpreted as a sign that 'value' – the price a seller can expect – has really increased.

Ideally, the most accurate way of quantifying strength of demand would be for the same coin, or similar coins, to be sold at regular intervals at the same auction house, when a price comparison should give a precise reading as to the increase or decrease in demand for that coin, or type of coin. This is, of course, rarely possible. The most practical approach in order to ascertain the current value of a coin is to find recent figures for others which are alike in as many respects as possible, and to make certain reasonable assumptions. If, for example, the coin you have is in F condition, but you can only find a recent price for one in VF, you may be able to find old prices for the coin in both grades, and thereby deduce a ratio of value between them. Assuming the figures were £75 in VF and £25 in F at a similar period some years ago, a current VF price of £225 would indicate £75 as correct for the coin in F condition. In fact, there is now a greater demand for quality than ever before, and, while this has led to only a slightly increased ratio between the lower grades, it is noticeably higher between VF and EF and markedly so between EF and UNC. This means that a comparison of this sort is valid only for lower-grade coins. Another reasonable assumption to make would be that coins of differing dates but of the same denomination, type and grade, are worth a similar amount. One must bear in mind, however, that no two coins are absolutely identical, and allow for the effect on value of any imperfections or enhancement which may differentiate two coins of the same grade. Also, where a rare coin was worth, say, five times the value of a more common one a number of years ago, it is reasonable to assume an *approximately* similar ratio of value today, provided that the two coins thus compared are similar in type. With dissimilar types, this may be entirely misleading, as trends in coin collecting, over a few years, can and do affect the values of certain types drastically, while others may not change at all.

Old sale catalogues and dealers' lists of coins for sale do therefore sometimes prove their usefulness, although it is clearly preferable to find a recent price and not have to resort to such devices in order to estimate value. A word of warning is appropriate on the danger of attaching too much significance to a single example. When a dealer offers for sale a coin he may have only once in a blue moon, he will probably be as much in the dark about how much to ask for it as anyone else would be: he may grossly under-rate the demand or go to the opposite extreme and try to make a killing with it by asking far too much. An auction is more likely to produce, approximately, the value of a very rare coin, and thus give a valid figure for future reference, although, as will be explained in Chapter 6, a particular auction or auction house may produce results which are not typical of the market. So, when researching in order to assess the value of a coin, rely less heavily on the evidence of a single example than on the results produced by a number of examples.

Be wary of attaching too much significance to the price of any coin described as having damage or other features which detract from its grading. Edge knocks have to be seen to be evaluated correctly: larger and more obvious knocks will matter, while insignificant blemishes on the edge may not. Scratches also vary substantially in their importance: if they are on the field – the area where there is no design – they are less serious than if on the face of the monarch.

It is advisable, when using old lists, to ignore figures put out by auctioneers or dealers who either are not specialists in coins or are not reputed to be accurate graders. Certainly anyone can make a mistake, but non-specialists have neither the expertise nor the reference books which are necessary to ensure consistent accuracy; and some individuals can be prone to exaggerations in grading, while others – rather fewer! – may be ultra-conservative.

There are even occasions when the established and reputable sources of information on coin prices are quite misleading, and prove the danger of assuming too much on the strength of one example. The fact that dealers – more often than is perhaps realised – do not sell coins on their lists is, hardly surprisingly, not publicised. When they have a particularly valuable coin, most will naturally try to take advantage of a rare opportunity and ask for more than they really expect, in the hope of finding a collector who is sufficiently keen to pay above the odds for it; or else they may be unfortunate enough not to find a buyer even when the coin is at the 'right' price. Whatever the reason, there are many instances of important coins reappearing on later lists or in auction catalogues, within a relatively short period after their first appearance. Such coins merit illustration, and any doubts that they are the same coins for sale can be dispelled by comparing photographs for marks which are distinctive. Dealers will want to avoid giving the impression that they cannot sell some coins, and consequently prefer to put them into auction, when the identity of the seller is not revealed, or else sell at a reduction to another dealer. No two have an identical clientèle and coins may pass through the hands of several dealers before they find a home in a collection. Just one example from many possible is the Sardinian gold Doppia of 1786 which a London dealer listed for sale at £2,200, but which four months later was knocked down at auction for £1,700. Even the latter figure may not represent the real value, as most expensive coins have a reserve price on them in auction, so that the seller can buy back rather than accept what he considers too low a figure. A coin which is in demand will show its true value in a good auction, but one which is not may have its value inflated by means of a seller's reserve artificially competing with a single bidder.

Another interesting fact which emerges when one compares photographs of coins for sale is the occasional reappearance of a coin being offered at a higher price than originally. If the interval between its appearances is a number of years, it is likely that the original buyer sold it back to the dealer; but how can one explain an increased price after only a few months, as is sometimes the case? Clearly, there is not, in so brief a period, time for the coin to have appreciated to the extent that there is sufficient profit both for the dealer to induce the buyer to sell back at more than the original retail price and then for him still to add a second margin of profit. The greater likelihood is that the dealer met a very good response, and realised he had priced the coin far too cheaply! Being unable to obtain other specimens readily, he would have withdrawn it from sale and informed would-be buyers that it was 'regrettably already sold'. The coin could then, after a decorous interval, be offered again at a much higher price, on the reasonable assumption that at least one potential buyer from before would still be willing to buy, at the higher price.

Whatever the conclusions you may wish to draw, it is clear that the value and strength of demand of any coin can most accurately be assessed when there are a number of specimens sold, and that it is dangerous to conclude too much from a single example.

Remember also that 'value', in practice, is only as much as you can get. On average, dealers pay one-third less than their selling price, perhaps less; they will never pay what they believe to be full value.

With cheap coins, they will want a much higher margin to justify their time and expense, whereas with expensive coins, they will still do handsomely with only a few per cent profit.

On the whole, auction room prices give a more accurate reflection of current value, as the notional value placed on a coin by a dealer is then replaced by a market value in its proper sense. Although an auction result will reflect only the limited interest of those present and/or those bidding, and not that of the entire coin world, at least it has the virtue of having been arrived at by being tested, hopefully, on a free and unfettered market.

False statistics

There are other ways in which the inexperienced may be misled by 'black and white' figures which are incorrect. Much reference is made to 'mintage figures' as a useful guide to rarity. While they often are, sometimes they are not. Although the period varies from one country to another, figures for quantities struck of coins over about one hundred years old must be regarded as generally unreliable. Officials occasionally falsified the records of coins struck and privately disposed of metal not coined; or, more often, the mintage figures recorded might include some coins struck that year but bearing the date of the previous year. This would save the bother of altering dies.

Although very rarely, official mintage figures of twentieth-century coins are occasionally distorted in this way; but such instances were authorised and freely admitted by officials. The problem is mainly with pre-twentieth-century coins. I was fortunate enough to have been in circulation at the same time as were post-1859 pennies of Queen Victoria, 60,000 of which I withdrew and amassed at random from currency. These are an interesting series, and very complicated, with a large number of varieties and different pairings of obverse and reverse. Apart from being able to date the commencement of generally accurate British Mint records to 1870, by comparison of these with what was, for all dates and most types, an adequate sample, I had as conclusive a foundation on which to base rarity estimates as ever can be possible, in the absence of irreproachable mint records. Prices are influenced substantially by availability, and paying too much or too little can be indicated by knowing how easy or how difficult a particular date or type is to obtain. Some dealers may quote mintage figures when it suits them to, and 'very rare' is an overworked epithet in the vocabulary of many. In the absence of reliable figures, one must be guided by the observations of those who have the most specialised experience – usually scholars or large dealers who keep careful records. Check with them or their books and you will not be misled.

Sometimes a planned issue of coins may be melted down before any or all have been released into circulation. Records may show quantities struck, but not quantities melted down, so here again experts and dealers have to make estimates. Some of the very rarest coins arise out of such circumstances, and there is always the possibility that someone sometime may discover, say, another Edward VIII threepence or 1933 penny. Not in the same category, but still scarce, are twelve-sided threepences of 1946, one of the best-known examples where the quantity struck is unknown: most of those struck in that year were dated '1945', but the mintage figures do not distinguish them from those dated '1946', recording only the total struck during the year.

It is of course time-consuming to research coins in lists and sale catalogues, and so much handier to be able to check up in one of the 'current price trend lists' which are available. These are popular for that reason, and, where there have been enough significant examples during the period of the survey, they will be accurate and useful. Unfortunately, in order to cover whatever groups of coins are being surveyed, they include many notional figures – guesses, based on old or insufficient examples – and these may be totally misleading. Few rare coins are priced as accurately as common ones, as prices remain unaltered or are very conservatively adjusted. One of the rarest and most important British coins, the 1877 farthing, is still quoted at £450 or £500 in mint state in such value lists, because no specimen has been auctioned for many years to prove this out-of-date estimate wrong, by about fifteen years and £2,000! Using the simple method of comparison already outlined, we find that, in 1978, a slightly less rare farthing of the same period – the 1860 in copper – realised £2,100 in auction, in EF condition. Prices of other important rarities in top grades have strengthened since then, so it becomes a safe assumption to say that a mint state 1877 farthing would be quite a bargain at £450–£500.

Further proof of the problems and inadequacies attached to valuing by guesswork was given by the value of £450 stated in the 1980 *Standard Catalogue of British Coins* for an EF penny of 1827, a rare date. If you had a specimen of this coin with a little lustre and no wear, you could, from the evidence of the catalogue, reasonably have been persuaded that an offer of £300 from a dealer would be fair. How wrong you would have been was shown by the fact that just such a coin fetched £1,200 in auction late in 1979, and it was bought by a dealer! EF is the highest grade for which a value is given for 1827 pennies in the catalogue – but, while not quite in mint condition, this particular coin was better than EF. The auction confirmed both the increased demand for such a coin, not anticipated by the cataloguers, who usually tend to err on the conservative side when they have to guess, and the importance of assessing accurately the condition of a rare coin in a high grade.

So beware of treating value lists as gospel. In the first place, let me repeat that they represent selling prices. Also, many of them will be, if not confirmed by actually having been sold, purely estimates. Even where they are backed up by plenty of examples, they may be out-of-date by the time you read them, and, in the same way as no two coins are identical, so values will differ in accordance with each nuance of condition.

Where you have to make a guess, do not underestimate the increased and increasing importance attached to almost any old coin in really choice condition. Even quite common ones, if really attractive, have appreciated far more than have very rare coins in lower grades. In 1968, for example, a London dealer offered a rare 1678 half-crown, GF/F, at £90, and the relatively common 1698 half-crown, nearly EF, at £12.50. By 1982 the value of the former, of which only between eleven and twenty specimens are believed to exist, had risen to about £200, whereas an EF 1698 half-crown was fetching almost £300!

The greatest emphasis on condition is put on coins of the United States of America, where the value of a perfect coin far exceeds that of even an almost perfect one. Even a common low-value coin such as the 1881 with 'S' mintmark silver dollar illustrates the point clearly:

UNC(MS-60)	UNC(MS-65)	UNC(MS-67)
$50.00	$109.00	$259.00

while a rarity like the 1884–S silver dollar really brings it home:

VF-20	EF-40	UNC(MS-63)
$34.00	$49.00	$8,495.00

Outside the United States, the tendency to put a premium on coins of superb quality is increasing, although to a less marked extent. That is the direction in which the market for all types of coin is moving, and that is where the wise investor looks for future gains.

5
Which coins should I buy?

The answer to the above question, to some extent, depends on whether you want, or are prepared, to put money into coins as a long-term investment, or to resell quickly for an immediate profit. Top-quality rarities are expensive, and both the general economic situation and the temporary shifting of demand to and away from particular types of coin may mean that their prices stagnate and they prove difficult to sell. This is a short-term problem only – demand may slacken temporarily but it is always there. Other, basically less desirable, coins may, on the other hand, have less long-term potential, but none the less present opportunities for short-term profits.

There is no hard-and-fast rule which will guarantee x per cent profit within a fixed period: there are greater and lesser degrees of likelihood over an approximate length of time, and the best one can do is to isolate and analyse the factors which apply, and to understand why and how they do.

As a long-term investment

The vast majority of people who buy coins are either collectors who specialise in collecting a particular type and limit their purchases accordingly, or else are those who might be described as 'magpies', buying attractive and interesting coins of various types, with little or no system of tie-up between them. For both groups, their principal concern with the financial aspect of a purchase will simply be a desire to pay less than the current value. Dealers who write on the subject of investment, almost without exception, are happy to encourage customers in thinking that they will also automatically make a good investment if they concentrate on collecting coins of whatever type interests them, in as good a condition as they can afford; and these dealers will seem to be right, because almost any collection kept for quite a few years is bound to be worth more than it cost. They specifically advise against buying coins for what one believes is their potential to appreciate.

Yet this is precisely what I am recommending to you. If you follow the advice of these dealers, luck may be on your side; but how much better it is to have reason and logic. The poker player who knows the odds and has studied the characteristics of the other players is unquestionably at an advantage over the player who simply likes the look of his hand or plays a hunch.

'Sitting on a collection is in fact no longer even a guaranteed investment, with high inflation and competitive interest rates now making it more necessary than ever before to cast a critical eye on the investment aspect of coin collecting. Without giving due consideration to this, the 'wrong coins' can mean a loss or, at best, an inefficient use of money. Over-the-board increases in value are no longer enough – selectivity is the answer. While one's own theories and reasoning may give guidance on the matter of which coins to buy, it must be sensible to study the facts by following the latest developments, by watching price movements both in auction and in dealers' lists. Persistent upward movement or a single dramatic jump must be clear indication of strengthening demand, while persistently stagnating prices or reductions, no matter how slight, indicate the opposite: most dealers would rather hold on to coins that do not sell than be seen to have to reduce their price. Would-be buyers tend to be discouraged from buying a coin which no one else wants, so dealers like to avoid giving the impression of this either by putting them into an auction, usually with a high reserve, or buy-back price, or by salting them away until such time as demand might have strengthened.

It is important not to misinterpret a hiatus as proof positive of low demand. All good investment coins reach temporary price peaks and 'rest' while the market may be said to 'catch its breath' – dealers may need time to sell out stock if a number of specimens of the same coin appear on the market at the same time, as may happen after a comprehensive specialist auction; or else dealers and/or collectors may consider a price excessive for a while, after a particularly sharp jump. If a coin is desirable, its price will not stagnate for long. There are never enough really desirable coins to satisfy long-term demand, with the result that stock of them is only a temporary and brief occurrence. A price pause will end when dealers are asked for coins they can no longer supply or obtain, and also once a record new high price becomes accepted as the norm.

Many older dealers and collectors find it hard to adjust to increasing prices as dramatic as some have been. They feel that today's prices are absurd, compared with those of yesteryear, and that the magnitude of the increases that have taken place precludes the possibility of anything comparable recurring. The effects of inflation similarly come as a shock to those with the longest memories, whereas youth has no preconceived notions as to what prices should be, based on remembrance of what they were.

Unlike that of most goods and services, however, the price of coins contains no element of manufacturing costs. Instead, it is based, almost exclusively, on the factors of supply and demand and the way in which they interact. There is no natural ceiling to the price of any coin, nor is there a cast-iron guarantee that prices will not fall to zero. When we attempt to forecast future trends in coins, what matters is whether or not the factors that contributed to today's prices still apply, whether they are likely to continue to apply, and whether there may be others likely to do so in addition. In theory, if all conditions remained identical, which of course they never do, one would have every reason to expect a steady and utterly predictable movement in price. The intrusion of a new factor will have a plus or minus effect on price movement, the direction of which – although not the extent – is easy to forecast.

To take an example, crown- or dollar-size silver coins, in better states of preservation, have been one of the best and steadiest investments over the last fifteen years. Few people outside the United States have ever used coins as large; hence they have a romantic 'olde worlde' appeal. They are spectacular because of their size and usually have much attractive and readily visible detail which smaller coins cannot exhibit to such effect. In short, they feel and look good! These factors cannot alter, so, although they are today more expensive than ever before, the factors which made them so persist and should continue to exert their influence to force prices up steadily.

The state of the economy might seem to be the principal and most obvious variable influence on coin prices; but this is rarely so. Certainly, those coins which one cannot buy without first checking one's finances have what might be called an 'investment aspect'. For a wealthy collector, this might apply to coins costing £5,000 or more; for others, perhaps £100 or less. Most gold, the more expensive crowns, and of course any other coins which make a dent in one's finances are subject to such an investment aspect, which affects their total sales, their demand, and thus their price. In a similar way, national prosperity boosts sales of luxuries: demand increases when there is more money about, and there is pressure to mark up prices of commodities of which demand exceeds supply.

So better coins do, and can be expected to, rise in price during times of general prosperity. But what about other times, unfortunately more frequent?

In times of crisis or instability, people place less trust in money and more in commodities of limited availability for which there is a fairly steady demand. When these conditions are extreme, this trend reaches epidemic proportions, and there is a rush to buy gold, the popular proven stand-by on such occasions. Most gold coins of the last hundred years or so, unless rare, are bought and sold as bullion – for their metal content – and not as collectors' items; so they rise and fall in price in a way other coins do not, predictable, if at all, only by reference to international finance and politics.

During times of minor depression or economic stagnation, investors see in coins, as in other antiques, a dependable and healthy alternative to industrial investment, with its poor rate of return. Their record is so good that confidence in good collectors' coins leads to an increase in demand for them. A major world recession, such as that occurring in the early 1980s, is, on the other hand, a different matter. With few exceptions, coins, like other commodities lacking a function, experience a general fall-off in demand. Money, being in short supply, is simply unavailable for less essential purposes, and, conversely, those who have it and who are willing to speculate on an early up-swing in the economy will find that many coins can be bought for substantially less than when business was good. What matters here is the unknown factor: how long will it be before the cheaply-bought investment increases in value? Ideally, the best time to buy is immediately prior to reflation, and on detecting early positive signs of economic recovery, which can usually be expected to initiate in America. In the absence of any encouraging signs, a price paid, however cheap, is likely to remain so or even fall further, if would-be purchasers are to be induced to buy. So don't buy if all is gloom and despondency!

Except during a major recession, in the short term attention may flicker from certain groups of coins to others, but coins in general are in demand, in bad times and in good.

The factor that most affects coin prices is not economic. While any coin which one considers expensive has to be bought with reference to one's finances, most coins are bought with only a glance at them. Collectors are motivated by an acquisitive desire which has a tendency to overrule economic logic. *The real key to a coin's price is strength of demand*, more than its availability, although the two are interconnected. Even a unique piece, if no one wants it, will be worthless. This seldom happens, but the sort of coin most likely to fall into this category would be a minor variety of a series which is not widely collected and in which there exist many minor varieties, in poor condition. Any unique coin with the opposite attributes will be worth a fortune! In between, there are many shades of importance. Two examples readily spring to mind where a reasonable degree of demand is overmatched by an abundance of supply, also resulting in very low values. These are Roman copper coins of the third and fourth centuries AD, which turn up in buried hoards in their thousands, and the British 'Churchill' crowns of 1965, almost 20,000,000 of which were struck, far too many for a collectors' item with no function as currency. Basically, old Roman coins, with great age and historical interest, and British crowns, an attractive and widely collected group of coins, are desirable, and, if only a few thousand existed, they would be valuable. As it is, a specimen of either can be purchased for under

A typical third-century Roman copper coin, except that such coins are seldom found in this condition. Emperor Quietus (AD 260–1), as struck, hence £300 (1977), but very substantially less for average and poor specimens

£1, and few dealers would pay anything like that if they bothered to handle them at all.

A good example illustrating just how pre-eminent is strength of demand over availability in determining value is the groat (four-pence) of Elizabeth I, which I once had, with the error spelling 'ELIZBETH'. Coins of this reign are popular and groats of Elizabeth are scarce, so I had high hopes that my coin, even although only in average condition, would prove valuable, especially as this error was unlisted and, probably, extremely rare. At auction, it fetched just what it would have done if it had been the normal coin. Although individually very rare, many mistakes in lettering occur on coins up to about 1660, and, in spite of apparently having so much in its favour, my groat was, in the last analysis, just another minor variety to the bidders.

Modern technology has made errors of this kind virtually im-possible. Instead, owing to the large numbers of coins needed today and the speed at which they have to be minted, flawed coins sometimes occur and, in spite of careful checking, occasionally pass into circulation. In Britain, freak coins still have to be appreciated for the rarities they are, but in America there is a market for them. One of the most blatant is the 1955 'double die' cent, which is not a great rarity but an unusual scarce error in a series where errors are uncommon. It sells for $1,000 in mint state. Perhaps the reason lies in the fact that the coin market in the United States is highly developed, and collectors of American coins who specialise have less to collect than do those of European coins, thus delving more deeply into the minutiae of their specialisation.

Coins prior to the seventeenth century were, as a rule, undated, and the advent of dated coins gave the collector of 'modern' coins his principal specialisation. If there is anything in the world of coins which makes good headlines, it is the discovery or sale of a rare-date coin, such as the 1933 penny, of which only eight are known. Almost everyone some time or another dreams of coming into money by a stroke of good fortune, and the idea of this possibly being attained through an 'ordinary' modern penny, until 1971 in circulation, makes the near-impossible seem a little less remote. Lesser, more affordable, rare-date coins are always in demand simply because there are many casual, as well as serious, collectors looking to complete a set of each year of whatever type they collect.

Where specialisations intersect, demand is substantially increased. To put it another way, a coin such as a rare type of Edward I penny will be wanted only by collectors of medieval penny types, whereas an Edward VIII crown of 1937 will be in demand by collectors of (a) British crown types, (b) crowns of each reign, (c) crown-size coins of each country, (d) coins of Edward VIII – admittedly there cannot be many! – and (e) investors in high-rarity and high-value coins. Even the rarest type of Edward I penny has a book value of only £350 in VF condition, while the potential demand for an Edward VIII crown is so immense that its value is estimated to be in excess of £40,000. There are, of course, many less spectacular examples to prove the point, and even such a coin as the 'Gothic' crown of 1847, of which some 8,000 specimens exist, commands a price of over £500 in EF condition. As most of these coins did not circulate, EF specimens are not difficult to find, and the price therefore reflects, not rarity, but strong demand for them. It is one of the most attractive and finely executed coins ever struck, and, belonging to a highly popular group, must be desired by very many thousands of collectors, world-wide, of whom, however, only some 5,000–6,000 or so have paid or are willing to pay £500 for an EF specimen. If there is an increase in the number of people who will pay this for one, the price rises until either sufficient owners are induced to sell or would-be buyers are deterred from buying, until an approximate equilibrium is reached between supply and demand.

It should be possible, based on the quantities known or estimated to exist, to categorise each coin as 'high-demand + high-supply', 'low-demand + high supply', 'high-demand + low-supply', and 'low-demand + low-supply', with gradations denoting the strength of the two factors contributing to the price. If this can be done with a reasonable degree of accuracy, by then comparing the actual prices of certain coins one can draw conclusions as to which coins are overpriced and which underpriced. Results in the middle must be inconclusive because one of the two factors – demand – cannot be quantified, but must instead be estimated on the basis of the coin's desirability; so only obvious instances of comparatively overpriced or underpriced coins should be considered reliable.

Dealers and shrewd investors draw general conclusions of this sort when they buy up and lay aside large amounts of those coins they believe to be ripe for appreciation. Usually what happens is that interest in a particular group of coins lags behind the demand for other groups, and the price ratio between them is altered to the extent that the group which has lagged behind seems cheap by comparison. So word gets around that so-and-so is buying up Cromwell silver, or Bolivian gold, or what-have-you, and sometimes demand is created simply by this act and news of it being spread around.

Specialisation is only one of the sources from which demand stems, and, with the influx of investors and new collectors in recent years, it is tending to have less bearing on strength of demand than it once did. Buying by investors is clearly orientated towards profit potential, irrespective of any other consideration; but profit potential, in the last analysis, is determined by the consumer – the coin collector – and what *he* wants is what a good investment will include.

Most new collectors – and many of long-standing – choose to buy coins which are visually attractive, interesting, and below a certain price. Only a dedicated collector or a confident investor will make what he considers to be an expensive purchase; and what constitutes that, besides always being a variable quantity, is constantly increasing, along with inflation and a general acceptance that most really worthwhile coins cost at least a few hundred pounds.

A 'pretty' coin appeals to everyone, and it may just happen also to be important to certain specialist collectors, whereas an unattractive one will only be in demand from specialists. We have already considered the appeal of crown- or dollar-size coins, resulting from their size and the amount of detail which can be portrayed on them. The same criteria apply to large gold coins – the five-guinea and five-pound piece – and to large copper coins – the penny, to take British examples. As a general rule, smaller coins are less popular.

With older coins, greater interest centres on those which portray famous historical personages, such as Julius Caesar, Cleopatra, Elizabeth I, Oliver Cromwell, and so on. Often their coins are the only true records of how they looked, and, where rare, enormous premium is placed on a choice-condition portrait coin.

From about AD 400 to 1500 the quality of coin design and manufacture was poor and many coins show only a stylised face of the monarch, crude and with features virtually indistinguishable from those of others of the period; hence there is no interest in them as portrait pieces and also little visual appeal. Coins of the Dark and

Hadrian (AD 117–38), an
exceptionally fine portrait
of an important emperor

Claudius (AD 41–54), silver cistophorus,
a superbly executed coin of importance
in top condition, EF, £2,200 (1977)

Gold guinea, William and Mary, 1689. Elephant and castle
below busts. Guineas are keenly collected by collectors of
gold and this coin is additionally desirable by having, unusually, two portraits (which make all coins of William and
Mary popular), and the emblem of the East India Company
below them; nearly EF, £850 (1977)

Middle Ages tend to derive the value they have from their degree of
rarity, their condition – with particular emphasis on how well they
were struck – and the importance of the denomination.

There are other designs, besides the portrait, which may enhance
the desirability of a coin. Any well-executed and artistic concept will
do this, but particular mention should be made of Ancient Greek
coins, where similar coins of similar rarity vary substantially in value
if one is the work of a superior artist. The finest of these are considered
never to have been surpassed, even to this day. Certain European
countries and states, from the sixteenth to the eighteenth centuries,
issued what are known as 'City talers', large silver coins which
depicted the buildings of certain cities as they were at the time; and
these are desirable because they provide a visual record of the town or
city at that date.

Oliver Cromwell, gold fifty shillings, 1656. All coins of the
'Protector' are popular and well struck. This is the highest
denomination of them, and only about twelve exist; slight
edge knock, otherwise nearly mint state, £17,500 (1978)

India (under Britain). A more recent restrike of a gold mohur,
William IV, 1835, the reverse of artistic and symbolic importance –
a fact that influences buyers attracted to coins with visual appeal;
EF and brilliant, £200 (1979)

Elizabeth I, silver crown, 1601, a coin always likely to be in demand with
a remarkable portrait of a famous queen and a large denomination; small
crack, otherwise nearly EF, £1,250 (1977)

Syracuse, silver tetradrachm, 275–215 BC,
nearly EF, £950 (1980)

Egypt (under Alexander the Great), c. 320 BC,
silver tetradrachm, GVF, £300 (1976)

Athens, silver tetradrachm, c. 450–420 BC, VF, £280 (1979)

Bold in style and bold in relief, the finest Greek coins are truly works of art.
As such, they have a wide appeal above and beyond the numismatic

---

All such coins can be appreciated by collectors and non-collectors
alike, and their appeal is not confined to the country in which they
originated. They have *international appeal*, which ensures high levels
of demand and thus value. Furthermore, they are not affected by
economic difficulties in the country of origin, as are most coins.

This point applies particularly to Ancient Greek and Roman coins,
which are collected everywhere, maintaining a fairly safe and steady
value. The only way in which this can be adversely affected is by the

Augsburg, Germany, 'City' taler, 1744, really GF, £300 (1980)

Venice, Italy, gold ten zecchini, 1700–9, one of the largest gold coins, and highly impressive, especially as EF, £4,500 (1976)

discovery of a hoard, which is not that rare an event. In times of strife, when plundering was widespread, individuals stood to lose everything they had. Wealth, in the form of gold and silver coin, would be buried or otherwise concealed, hopefully to be retrieved once the danger had passed. When they died, the secret of where they hid their wealth often died with them. Towards the end of the Roman Empire, many such hoards seem to have been buried, as many thousands of Roman coins from the late third and fourth centuries AD have been, and continue to be, found over most of the area once ruled by Rome. There tend to be, in each hoard, coins of similar type, and their appearance on the coin market in quantity has a depressing effect on the price of that type. Hoarding was also prevalent at certain periods of the Dark and Middle Ages, and the discovery of large quantities of silver pennies from the reign of Stephen (1135–54), when there was civil war in England, lowered the auction price of average specimens from £70 in 1975 to £35 in 1980. Shipwrecks too have contributed to the supply of certain coins, notably Spanish-American gold and silver of the seventeenth and eighteenth centuries, although many have been corroded, in varying degrees, by long immersion in seawater.

The lesson for the investor, if there is any, is that the rarity of any really old coin is not absolutely guaranteed, whereas with most modern coins, it is safe to assume no sudden sharp increase in the quantities available. Although it can be a disappointment to find that a coin for which one has paid highly many years ago is now available for less, it is important to keep this in perspective and point out that, out of the multitude of coin types issued over the centuries, only a few are affected in this way. The one safe bet is that the market for early coins in *really choice condition* will not deteriorate, so long as there are coin collectors. Amazingly, some hoards do produce coins in exceptional condition, but these are always snapped up without reducing the value; and the vast majority of hoards show the ravages of time.

In Chapter 2, the importance of grading and its effect on value was discussed. Now, in determining what makes some coins more desirable than others, it is the right place to assert that condition is *the principal* factor involved. Any mint-state coin is more attractive, and therefore more desirable, than any worn coin, except to those who happen to know that the worn coin is much rarer – so much so, that the secondary factor of rarity supersedes the primary one of condition.

Threepence, George VI, 1949, a scarce date, worth about £1 in average condition, but a real rarity when truly uncirculated, £100 (1976)

The shift of emphasis from rarity to condition is a relatively recent phenomenon, and it is ever-increasing, so that it is clearly on the cards to forecast price increases for most choice coins. Demand has always been high for them, but the price ratio between UNC. and EF, and between EF and VF, is steadily increasing.

Using some of the examples from the Seaby Index, which are the dealer's selling price, this point is brought out:

	HENRY VII, Sovereign			ELIZABETH I, Pound (Mintmark 'O')	
	F	VF		F	VF
1974	£2,500	£4,000	1974	£200	£375
1975	5,000	9,000	1975	750	800
1976	5,000	10,000	1976	750	1,000
1977	5,500	12,000	1977	750	1,250
1978	6,500	13,000	1978	800	1,750
1979	7,500	15,000	1979	1,000	2,500
1980	7,250	15,000	1980	1,000	2,500
1981	8,000	16,500	1981	1,200	2,750
1982	7,500	17,500	1982	1,000	2,750

WILLIAM III, Crown, 1696, 1st bust

	F	VF	EF
1974	£11	£32.50	£75
1975	16	60	200
1976	20	70	250
1977	20	72.50	265
1978	22	75	400
1979	22	90	500
1980	30	105	—
1981	30	120	—
1982	30	120	600

GEORGE IV, Shilling, 1821

	VF	EF	UNC.
1974	£7.50	£17.50	£30
1975	8	25	40
1976	10	30	50
1977	11	32.50	55
1978	12.50	35	65
1979	15	47.50	80
1980	15	47.50	—
1981	18	60	—
1982	18	65	120

VICTORIA, Crown, 1845

	VF	EF	UNC.
1974	£20	£100	£300
1975	30	160	400
1976	32.50	175	475
1977	35	200	600
1978	35	200	700
1979	47.50	335	1,000
1980	50	425	—
1981	65	475	—
1982	50	500	1,250

These few examples are far from representative, but they do illustrate certain pertinent points. Coins of Elizabeth I, even in lower grades, are in demand – especially those showing her portrait in detail, with elaborately jewelled dress, ruff, and flowing hair. Most coins of Victoria have a similar appeal, although their greater availability has limited the extent to which their value has risen in this period. Any coin with a good clear portrait of one of history's most prominent 'characters' has done particularly well. William III is no more notable, in this respect, than any other monarch of recent centuries, nor are his coins, as a group, rare. What the statistics for the 1696 crown indicate is, therefore, that demand for lower-grade crowns, if it has increased at all over this period, lags far behind demand for choice ones. The increases for the coin in F and, to a lesser extent, in VF are attributed solely to the pull of the EF price, comparison with which made them seem cheap. Facts such as this tend to be overshadowed by the spectacular rises of EF coins. Although crowns may lead the way, sharp value rises have occurred for virtually all choice coins prior to 1800, and for many nineteenth-century coins also. Just how common low-grade coins are, by comparison, cannot properly be appreciated until one looks through the 'junk' trays – and even the 'better coin' trays – which dealers have. A low price is what sells such coins, whereas price is a secondary consideration to the collector who wants a better-grade specimen.

The 1821 shilling is of a type which was struck that year only, and is therefore an important coin to shilling collectors. Potentially, it is a high-demand coin, especially in UNC. condition, yet the price increase from 1974 to 1979 was 'only' fourfold, the lowest for any of these five examples. Shillings, and sixpences, are in much lower demand than crowns or any other large coins; hence the increases, generally, on a much lower scale. Also, while important to the specialist shilling collector, the non-specialist may well prefer more common or more interesting coins than small silver of the unimportant George IV, especially as he can buy a shilling of 1826 for much less, if he wants one of this reign and is not concerned about which type he has.

As is obvious, the Henry VII sovereign is in a class of its own. The first and rarest sovereign, a popular coin, very few appear for sale, and even fewer are tested in auction to establish what would be an accurate value. These figures are largely a guess, based on perhaps a single negotiated sale during what is accepted as a poor period for hammered gold. In the long term, classic rarities cannot fail to appreciate well, and during 1980 there was ample evidence of much-increased demand in the record prices being paid for coins in this price bracket, although, since then, there has been slight slackening of demand in the face of a deep recession.

A general survey of price movements for the various groups of English coins is made by the London dealer, B.A. Seaby Ltd, and published every two or three months in *The Daily Telegraph* by John Pearson Andrew. Although the survey reports are insufficiently long to deal with the specific, they do give an up-to-date and authoritative résumé of the way in which coin prices are moving; and this type of information is of great relevance to those about to buy or sell coins.

The coin market in the United States is so far advanced in development as to justify a weekly publication which gives the very latest prices for American coins. The volume of trade there far exceeds that in any other country, and the accelerating demand for top-quality coins was made obvious by a report from an American dealer to the effect that, between August 1979 and May 1980, their prices for MS-65 specimens (almost perfect uncirculated) over a wide range of US coins increased, on average, by 152 per cent, or just over $2\frac{1}{2}$ times. Perhaps dealers encouraged or over-anticipated the market for expensive coins, as, in many instances, prices since then have returned almost to their 1979 levels.

Suddenly, by comparison, non-US coins seemed cheap, and, both as a result and in anticipation of corresponding price rises for foreign coins, American dealers and investors bought heavily abroad. As always, the gains were most decisive among top-condition coins with an 'international appeal'. The trend is definitely towards selectivity in the American style, although not yet with its numerical subdivision of grades, as prices for 'choice uncirculated' coins race ahead of those for coins with even a slight imperfection. Lesser increases can be expected for coins which are in lower demand, more in sympathetic reaction than anything else, when the gap between them and better coins has become so wide that they seem to be underpriced.

It certainly pays to follow the latest trends abroad as well as at home, and the significance of developments in the United States should not be underestimated. Being the wealthiest nation in the world, and having many more coin collectors than any other single country, it is logical that the highest prices should be paid for the most desirable American coins, and that the strength of its demand, when exerted, should have a world-wide effect.

The economic condition of any country has a bearing on the demand for, and thus the price of, its own coins, because most coin collectors collect coins of their own country, and because how much they pay for them depends on how much they have available to spend. Consequently, in varying degrees, there is strong demand and good potential for good coins of Japan, Canada, Australia, Switzerland, Britain, Germany, Sweden, Holland, and various others. A dramatic example illustrating just how much the price of a desirable coin can jump, when there is an upsurge of interest in a previously neglected area, is the Australian half-sovereign of 1866 which realised A$1,400 in 1977 and A$31,000 three years later. Political and economic renaissances in Spain and modern Greece have also led to an increased demand for coins of these countries, and important coins of both have appreciated substantially in recent years. It may be possible, from their example, to predict where opportunities to profit may lie from the buying of coins originating from a country with improving economic prospects. The revival of interest in Islamic culture and history has similarly had an effect on demand for the more important Islamic coins.

At the other end of the scale, in Communist countries and the poorer or underdeveloped areas of South America, Africa and Asia, there is no opportunity for the populace as a whole to indulge in coin collecting to any marked extent. There is, however, outside the countries of origin, demand for old coins from those which are of historical importance. These include Tsarist Russia, pre-Communist China, colonial Spanish-America, and the former British Empire. The larger denomination coins in, as always, EF condition or better, and the rarest main types and dates are avidly sought. With international demand, their prices are not affected by the current economic condition of these areas. The vast majority of coins from countries with very large populations, such as China, India, and Russia, are likely to have been struck in such quantity as to be available far in excess of demand, and consequently have little value and little likelihood of appreciation unless an economic miracle occurs.

By and large, those coins which are going to be valuable in the future already are. What is more open to speculation is the extent to which their value will increase and at what rate this will occur. Nevertheless, the public is susceptible to the attractive appearance and 'limited issue' allure of modern commemorative proof issues, struck for the purpose of cashing in on the market for collectables. The large majority of these issues are not coins in the true sense – intended for use as currency – and their limited availability cannot enhance their value, as is claimed by those who strike and issue them, unless demand exceeds that limited availability. Too often the issuing government strikes more than potential demand can justify, sells at too high a price, or overestimates demand, with the result that prices fall and those who bought them cannot resell except at a loss. The least hazardous of these have been low mintage issues from a country which enjoys world-wide popularity with collectors, or from one with an active collector/dealer market. Because most of them are recent issues, what observations can be made apply only to the short term; but even in the long term, perhaps the example of the American commemorative half-dollars gives us our best insight into the future prospects of such issues. Dating back to 1892, with dozens of different issues at intervals over the following sixty years, only the rarest have become valuable. Demand for choice and rare current coins, on the other hand, has increased by leaps and bounds; and what demand there is for US commemoratives is more likely to stem from the fact that they are US issues, tapping a unique and enormous market, than from the intrinsic importance of each issue, which is superficial. Similar issues from any other country would have fared much worse, and the prospects for issues of more recent times, from far less important countries, cannot be viewed with any great degree of enthusiasm.

The most common pitfall for the inexperienced to avoid is the danger of overestimating the demand for 'average' coins. The vast majority of coins available to collectors are badly worn and common. They are not wanted now, nor are they likely to be. This includes most currency of the last hundred years or so which, owing to the rapid increases in population and trading opportunities, was in constant use. It also includes certain other coin types such as the heavy British copper issues of 1797–1807, late Roman copper, etc., in the lowest grades.

By comparison, all other coins look good, and therein lies the danger. Many ordinary collections consist of average coins – usually common modern-date sets in VF or EF, or low-denomination old coins in the lower grades. Auctions sell such coins in lots of several hundred at a time, and, unless a lot includes a particularly rare coin, the average individual price works out very low indeed. Nor has the collector any option when he wants to sell. Most dealers are simply not interested, and those who might have been can buy similar coins at auction for a fraction of the price the collector has paid for them, if he bought them from a dealer. The idea of owning a silver penny of the thirteenth century, showing clearly the head and titles of Edward I, may be attractive; but they are, as a group, very common, and available in auction for relatively little. The inexperienced buyer can be, and too often is, over-impressed by the age of a coin and by what enthusiasm or veneration it may arouse in him. On the other hand, he will often be surprised by the apparent insignificance of a coin which is really important. Subscribing to magazines and dealers' lists will help to remedy a deficiency in knowledge; but auction catalogues, with prices realised, give the best indication of value.

There are times when dealers will not be keen to buy even good coins – unless at a bargain price. If the dealer has a lot of money tied up in a large or expensive stock, and business is not as brisk as he anticipated, he will not be in a position to buy more, unless he knows he can resell immediately, either because he already has a customer waiting for such a coin, or because he paid so little for it that, even after his profit is added, it will still be a bargain and therefore be snapped up. Normally the state of the coin market is such that dealers will turn away some good coins offered to them at a fair price, but keenly advertise for others. Coins are never available in just the proportions that dealers and collectors would like. There may be a glut of rare Greek dekadrachms, perhaps after a large specialist sale or when a small hoard has been discovered. Selling a coin worth thousands of pounds is not an everyday event for most dealers, and, sensibly, they will try to carry a varied stock in order to satisfy a wide spectrum of collector demand. It can be very advantageous to note which coins appear on dealers' 'wants' lists, as well as those which are rising in price steeply on dealers' lists or at auction. These will be high-demand coins and easy to sell at a good price. If you have some which are difficult to sell at a fair price, it is best to hold on to them: if there is a basic demand for them, the time will come when dealers' stock will dwindle and they will be glad to be offered your coins.

When demand is low, or supply exceeds it, this can be recognised easily. Most dealers will be stuck with coins of the same type, or else the same coin may be offered for sale on several occasions. Dealers naturally prefer to extol the virtues of their coins, and the only time you will learn from them just how little they want to buy, and therefore how keen they really are to sell, is when you offer them coins of similar type and quality to their stock, at a price which would allow them a reasonable profit margin. It is probably wrong to assume, from seeing rare or valuable coins on a dealer's list, that he would be interested in buying such coins: he may not be able to find a buyer and have a lot of money tied up as a result. What he is more likely to want are choice coins of a type he does *not* have. It is always easier to notice objects present in a room than those which are absent. When no dealer has any stock of a high-demand coin, that is the time when a record price will be paid as soon as a specimen becomes available. So be aware of what the dealers need rather than what they have.

As a short-term investment

Much of what applies to long-term coin investment also applies to short-term. What makes a coin intrinsically desirable does not alter. The main differences concern the economics involved: how prices of coin types vary in their movement, and which are more likely to be profitable in the long run than the short.

The longer you hang on to a coin, the better will be your chances of selling it at a profit. If you paid a bit more than you needed to, or sell it for less than you could have, you should still not lose, given a lapse of a few years at least between buying and selling: the margins for inefficiency are widened by the passage of time, because coin prices generally tend to drift upwards. It is always important not to overpay or undersell, and especially so when interest rates are high and your money could be more gainfully deployed than in coins. Contrary to the impression usually given by most writers on the subject, the majority of coins do not increase in value sufficiently to compete with interest rates or other potential investments, at such times.

The need to be selective in what one buys and how much one pays is always present, but, if short-term profits are to be made, it becomes imperative. More care and thought must go into each transaction, as mistakes cannot be erased with the assistance of inflationary trends, as is otherwise the case.

Dealers' profits, for the main part, emanate from retail sales to their collector customers. Purchases may either come from auction, in competition with other dealers and at least a few keen or knowledgeable collectors, or else from over-the-counter, when the few good coins which appear are usually offered for sale by collectors who know their value and expect to receive an amount not far short of it. On average, a dealer will add 50 per cent on to his cost to arrive at a retail price, which is the same as saying he pays a third less than his selling price. In theory! All prices are notional and most negotiable. For a start, the margin of profit is whatever he can make it: rather more on what he considers to be a low-value coin simply to make it worth his while bothering with it, and less on a high-value coin – 5 per cent on £5,000 is as good as 50 per cent on £500. Also, what one dealer considers to be an expensive coin may be 'chicken-feed' to another. Consequently, a large dealer may well be doubling his outlay when he sells a coin at £100, while a small one may only be making £15 or £20. The conclusion must be that smaller dealers pay better for lower-price coins. For high-value coins, on the other hand, it must be better to sell to a large dealer: he is far more likely to have as his customers the few who can afford to buy expensive coins. The small dealer may have one or two, but he cannot lay out large sums of money on the off-chance that he may find a customer. When a small dealer does buy an expensive coin, he has to *know* he can resell it at a profit, and this means normally that either he is buying it very cheaply or else he knows someone – usually another dealer – who is looking for that very coin.

Immediate or short-term profit-taking is the aim of all dealers, except with coins which they believe to be undervalued and ripe for a steep increase. There is clearly only a marginal profit to be made, at best, when dealers buy and sell amongst themselves. How much chance, then, is there for non-dealers to compete successfully in buying coins to resell quickly at a profit? Very little, or so it would appear.

The way in which it can be done is to know a little more – the very advantage dealers have over the public and casual, or half-interested, collectors who may offer them coins – and thus not miss bargains; and to reach collectors when selling.

Most dealers do not have time to specialise, but have a reasonable working knowledge of value for most types of coins. Consequently, by having more detailed knowledge of certain types, it is possible for anyone to identify a coin for sale at a bargain price because the dealer is not aware of its full potential. Opportunities of this sort will usually arise where the coin is a rare variety or an unidentified foreign type.

No one can possibly specialise in every branch of as large a subject as coins, and the real key to short-term profits is to be versatile, to be alert to any opportunities which may present themselves, and to seek them out actively. The criterion here is not whether a coin has potential to appreciate, but whether or not it is sellable at a profit now.

Desirability, and the factors which affect it, remain constant. They have already been analysed and they apply to supply and demand in the short term also. However, there are times when it can be profitable to buy and resell very common or ordinary coins, those in mediocre condition and which few serious collectors would consider buying.

A fairly recent phenomenon is the marketing of coins, attractively packaged and presented, direct to the general public. The jewellery trade has always bought gold coins for conversion into rings, etc., and the cheaper the cost to the manufacturer, the higher his profit: hence demand for common dates and lower grades. Silver threepenny-bits and farthings are also used for the same purpose, so, while average specimens of common dates are not in demand from collectors, jewellers will buy them in quantity. Now, the gift market includes pre-decimal currency coins, purchased and packaged at little cost, presented as 'collectors' items'. Common and low-grade crowns also look quite impressive to most people, when they are set in an attractive perspex, or similar, container. Such coins, being readily available in quantity, cannot appreciate almost every time they appear on the market, as unusually choice or rare coins do; but there is an immediate profit for the entrepreneur who knows where to buy and where to sell. Silver coins of 1887, struck to commemorate the Golden Jubilee of Queen Victoria's reign, are very common, and, because so many people kept them as souvenirs of the event, even today they frequently turn up in excellent condition. As a consequence, worn specimens can be bought very cheaply – to the surprise of non-collectors, who tend to equate value with age. When one coin of each denomination is set in a modern case, the result can be quite impressive – indeed, positively exotic compared with modern cupro-nickel coins similarly packaged. The public does not know for how little the coins may be bought from a dealer or at auction, and willingly accepts the price asked for what is presented as an important set and a good investment. If the bullion price of silver rockets to such an extent that it actually surpasses the selling price of such 'sets', in that unlikely event, they would show a profit to those who buy them.

Even the common 'bun' and 'veiled' head pennies of Victoria, worn to the point of being almost indecipherable, have a market. In 1966, by when I had amassed some 60,000 of them, I found a dealer who was willing to pay $2\frac{1}{2}$ times their face value, plus freight charges. Nowadays, with inflation, I see similar pennies in dealers' trays at 15p or 20p each – about forty times face value. Although most dates are quite easily obtained in worn state, the public has a soft spot for Victoriana, and coins of her reign are always popular.

It would be wrong to conclude, from the above, that almost any coin is potentially profitable in the short term with the addition of selling expertise. Candidates must be cheap to buy so that they will not be too expensive to sell; must be in reasonably good condition, so that they are identifiable; and no longer be available in circulation, so that any degree of rarity or investment potential claimed cannot be refuted first-hand. Especially suitable would be long-discontinued denominations, such as silver groats (fourpences), guineas and crowns, of the eighteenth and nineteenth centuries. Older coins, apart from being too expensive generally to allow a large profit, are normally less well-struck and thus less attractive to the layman; and many old coins have designs and lettering which are not clearly understood or identifiable to the public.

There are, no doubt, still many unexploited opportunities for cheap coins to be bought and sold profitably. Whatever these may be, they involve marketing technique more than anything else. And their appeal, or, more correctly perhaps, the inducement to buy them, has to stem from their low price, rather than any intrinsic 'collector appeal'. Millions of people have, over the years, amassed – 'collected' is too strong a word! – a small cache of coins, and, as every dealer well knows, this almost invariably consists of badly worn, common, and almost worthless coins. Each of these people harbours illusions that his collection includes important and valuable coins, and believes that the dealer is concealing the truth when he makes a very low offer, in the hope of acquiring them cheaply. While this is not impossible, the truth usually is that coins of similar type can be bought anywhere at any time, and the dealer, with his wider experience, sees what the amateur does not.

That there is any demand at all for common or low-grade coins is because there are always young or new collectors eager to own, perhaps, a 2,000-year-old coin, or whatever intrigues them, and who are more concerned with actually having the coin than with its quality or resale potential. In time, when a collector has become more committed to his hobby, he will recognise the desirability of being more selective, both with regard to forming a coherent collection, as opposed to having a hotch-potch, and to condition, which entails paying more for his coins. The further each collection advances, the more sophisticated and selective become the requirements of its owner, and the more difficult it is for dealers to sell him something. Most dealers carry sufficiently varied a stock to achieve a fair percentage of sales from their potential customers, and have no need actively to seek out particular coins, unless they are valuable and there is a customer looking for them, when it will be worthwhile to do so. The dealers' stocks vary with the opportunities which arise to buy saleable coins at profitable prices. The only coins dealers *need*, and for which they will reduce their profit margin and pay well, are those which collectors want and cannot obtain. This is true for all dealers, and it reinforces the point that only the very choice or very rare coin, when bought retail, can be easily resold at anything approaching its full value.

Coins which are important and rare do not become less so – the opposite, in fact, as the number of collectors increases. What may diminish for a while is their rate of appreciation as investments. Experience has shown this only to be a temporary feature, and, even when demand is slack, prices often drift upwards, merely as a reaction to the price movement of comparable coins, which make them seem cheap. Almost inevitably there will be a resurgence of interest, when prices will really leap forward and compensate for the long 'sleep'.

English hammered – i.e. pre-1663 – gold is a case in point. From 1974 until 1979 prices stagnated after having climbed steadily. During that period, interest focused on later, milled gold. Five-guinea and five-pound pieces of the rarer types, in EF condition and better, as might be expected, showed particularly sharp increases, although, at the other extreme, the cheapest gold coins were also highly successful, owing to a period of hectic demand for bullion gold. This had the effect of nudging up prices generally, so that the traditional differential between specific types was maintained. By 1979 it was obvious that earlier gold was, by comparison, very cheap, and when, early in 1980, a Henry VII Ryal, of which only eight specimens are known, came up for sale in auction, it realised the surprisingly good price of £6,000, although it was cracked and only in F condition. This acted like a signal to the coin market. With confidence restored in hammered gold, further record prices were realised a few months later, for top-quality Tudor and Stuart gold, basically the most sought-after group within this type because of its often rare and unusual denominations and pleasing designs. A particularly attractive coin, a Ryal of Elizabeth I, which was estimated to realise £8,500, fetched £22,000, a surprise even to the auctioneers, who sometimes tend to be conservative in their published estimates.

As was reported in *The Daily Telegraph*, with reference to the Seaby Price Index, those people who had bought hammered gold coins in 1974 had, by 1979, lost money in real terms. No worthwhile investment, during a period of high inflation, gives a zero return. What is now clear is that, when certain groups of coins show massive or sustained price increases, the imbalance resulting is bound to become obvious sooner or later and will be rectified by increases, probably less dramatic, in the prices of other coins which lag behind.

So, any group which has stagnated for a period *may* be about to improve rapidly. At the time of writing, modern coins have been 'asleep' for quite a few years, so there is no regular pattern to allow predictions to be made. However, it is reasonable to assume that any coins which have been popular but have gone out of favour will regain their popularity, the likelihood increasing the further their prices lag behind. No short-term gains here, unless you are lucky enough to buy just prior to the up-swing.

For most people the choice is not so much whether to buy coins to hold for a number of years or for early resale, as whether to lay out money on several cheaper coins or one really good one. It is pointless to consider investing in coins unless you are prepared to lay out a minimum of about £100. There are few top-quality coins of high-demand types available for less than this. As a rough guide, the highest percentage increases occur with coins in the £100–£500 range, so, if you are restricted to such an amount as your investment, one good coin should be better than a number of inferior ones. If you have a larger amount available, on the other hand, look to choice coins within this range rather than pricier ones above it for the highest rates of appreciation. Beyond £500, the number of potential buyers decreases, ever more sharply the higher one goes.

This advice must be tempered by mention of important exceptions. It is still possible to buy choice copper and bronze coins for under £100, and it is impossible to buy decent, pre-1887, high-denomination gold for under £500. A two-guinea piece costing that amount is almost certain to be in inferior condition and a most unlikely investment. The correct comparisons to make are between mint-state coins at different price levels: all choice specimens can be recommended, but the preference should be for those within this range.

As with all investments, nothing is a certainty, and anyone who writes or says otherwise is either mistaken or a charlatan. What can now be judged, and could not be ten years ago, is the degree of probability which can be assumed in price movements, based on trends and patterns which have been observed since coins became widely accepted as genuine investment material. Following these trends and patterns can be likened to buying shares in large, established companies; but, as in industry or commerce, there can emerge from obscurity a group of coins which were undervalued and which surprise the pundits by suddenly showing rapid and substantial appreciation. There is no uniformity about coins: each one differs from another, however minutely, and both demand for different types and the price range within which demand is greatest vary from one area to another and even from one dealer to another in the same area. The tastes, the means, and the opportunities available to collectors and dealers all influence the demand for and supply of each type of coin, and they vary between New York and Cairo just as they do between Fifth Avenue and the Bronx. Generalisations are not rules and, as we have seen, opportunities do exist with even the most menial of coins.

I have tried to identify those factors which mark out a coin as a candidate for good investment, and to distinguish between those coins which can be expected to appreciate with some degree of reliability and others, which may enjoy a temporary spell of popularity but otherwise stagnate.

What you have read so far has no practical value without also the knowledge of how to put it to use. The next step is to consider when and where to buy and sell, and how to set about it.

6

How, when and where to buy and sell

A modest millionaire once said that the key to his success was to be in the right place at the right time. There is little point in having all the 'right' coins without knowing how to sell them to best effect: a bargain price you may have paid for a coin you cannot sell is no bargain, and equally, paying a high price can still be profitable if you can correctly anticipate when and where an even higher price will be paid.

Apart from going out and by luck digging them up, the cheapest way to acquire coins is to take advantage of the seller's ignorance of their real value. This can be done in many ways, and no doubt the question of the morality involved can be raised. As a corollary, the dearest way also stems from ignorance – on the part of the buyer. The long-term investor will be far more concerned that he has the right coins than whether or not he bought or sold for the optimum benefit, because the net result, if the coins prove to be the right ones, will involve a handsome profit regardless of the percentage lost by some degree of overpaying or underselling. For the dealer, on the other hand, or the short-term investor, with the necessity of working on smaller margins, finding the right source of supply and selling where he can obtain the best price is of paramount importance. If you have to rely on buying from knowledgeable people all the time, the pickings will be poor indeed, and inevitably the seller's knowledge will sometimes be greater than your own, with sad consequences.

So, at one extreme there is the possibility of buying from members of the public who may have been given their coins as a gift or have found them at the back of a drawer, with neither the knowledge nor the need to sell wisely in order to make a profit; and, at the other, of buying from dealers who, very definitely, have the need, and are most likely to have the knowledge, with the outcome more probably to the dealers' advantage than to yours.

Coins which are important have, for the most part, already been identified as such and will either already be in the possession of a collector or else in dealers' trays. The chance of picking up a bargain in a general antique shop still exists, as it does in a 'junk' assortment in a coin shop or at auction; but, discounting the odd stroke of luck, one has to look to the collector who wishes to sell, in order to buy collectable coins profitably. So where does the collector sell? Possibly privately, which will probably benefit the buyer; possibly to a dealer, which will almost certainly be to the advantage of the dealer; and possibly in an auction, where the benefit may lie with either buyer or seller.

As a purchase and a sale are opposite aspects of one and the same transaction, instead of looking at all the pros and cons from each side separately, it will be simpler to consider each possibility from both sides and state where any advantage to either is likely to be.

The private transaction

A private transaction eliminates direct competition, with agreement on a price reached by discussion. The absence of competition must benefit the buyer, except in the rare instances where his enthusiasm to acquire a particular coin is obvious and the seller can hold him to ransom, or where the buyer wrongly assesses the grade, type, or current value. These situations occur when the seller has to be induced to sell, and where, therefore, negotiations are initiated by the would-be buyer. It is more normal for collectors to sell when *they* decide to, and opportunities of the kind mentioned can thereby be missed.

Many become so attached to the idea of owning a particular coin that they fail to spot and take advantage of a situation where a keen buyer offers them a very high sum for it. Somehow psychology over-rules logic: 'He wants it badly; I have something he wants badly; I won't sell.' Perhaps this way of thinking, in a perverted way, helps to give a boost to an ailing ego, and, of course, in other instances, the owner simply intends not to sell at all. If, however, the intention is to sell at some time or another, which is usually the case, the interest of a potential buyer increases the desirability of the coin, in the mind of the owner, and logic goes by the board. He fails to see an opportunity which may not recur when he is looking to sell.

The normal situation is where the owner is first to express his wish to sell. If he does not know of a collector interested in the coin, he may choose to put the word around either verbally, as in a coin club, or else advertise in a magazine or paper. The onus of deciding the price, or the negotiable price range, is then on the shoulders of the seller, with the inherent disadvantages this entails. Generally coin collectors over-estimate poorer-quality coins and underestimate better specimens. Both in real terms and proportionately, the price gaps are widening, with the result that collectors who have had their coins for a long time and who are not fully in touch with the latest market trends, will have difficulty in selling their poorer coins and sell their better ones too cheaply. If they know what they are doing, they will sell efficiently, provided they can find buyers.

Reversing the situation, the well-informed buyer should have opportunities to obtain good coins reasonably from collectors who are trying to sell; but not from the 'hard to get' brigade, for whom normal financial motivation does not operate.

Buying from and selling to dealers

Here, transactions will take place solely on the basis of whether or not they are, or look as though they will be, profitable for the dealer. Perhaps the odd dealer savours the power of being able to refuse to buy or sell for reasons other than financial; and others may change their prices according to the means of, or discount terms expected by, whoever walks through their door.

On the basis that any price they may offer is liable to be negotiable and therefore not genuine, it is advisable to avoid such dealers. Many good dealers will be quite prepared to buy back what they sell, at a third less. While this is not much use if you hope to gain from the transaction, at least you can derive confidence from the fact that the dealer does not believe he is making a killing from the sale. Frankly, buying from a knowledgeable dealer offers little opportunity to the investor in the short term; and long-term profitability depends on buying the right coin and knowing where to sell it to obtain as good a price as possible.

When a dealer buys from you, he is most unlikely to pay as much as a collector will, for any coin, and, where a collector might well buy cheap or low-grade coins, many dealers will simply not be interested. The only occasion when a dealer may pay as much or even more than collectors is when the coin is particularly choice or important and is thus certain to appreciate, and at a time when it has perhaps not risen in price for some time. The dealer will then be anticipating an early price increase, and, because the coin is in demand and because he is in touch with many collectors and other dealers, some of whom will want the coin, he can be confident of at least getting his money back if he sells it.

Dealers have the advantage over all except the specialist collector, and are bound to subscribe to magazines and receive lists of coins for sale at auctions and in other dealers' trays, thus keeping in touch with the latest developments on the subject of prices and availability. Also, without the element of competition, when a seller approaches a dealer, the latter will often refer authoritatively to the 'flat market' for this type of coin and the difficulty in selling it, etc., or down-grade its condition; and such denigrating comments, together with a take-it-or-leave-it attitude can induce a trusting collector to accept what his research or logic tell him to be too low a price.

Auctions

It is precisely this element of competition which distinguishes the auction from the private sale or a sale to the trade. Not only are dealers and others forced to show their hand by having to bid to their limit, or near to it, but also their confidence and the desirability of the coins being sold are often both enhanced by the sight and sound of others buying. This tends to apply more to some collectors whose enthusiasm, on occasion, can overrule their common-sense, although dealers are not always immune.

Auctions are where most trading in coins occurs, and an enormous quantity changes hands through them, from various sources. There are, however, different categories of auction, and these can be assessed from the status they enjoy, their degree of specialisation, or geographical location, and the differences in type of customer and prices for coins which result.

A general auctioneer whose trade is normally selling furniture, paintings, and the more usual wares of the antique shop, may sometimes have in a sale a few coins, tucked away under 'miscell-aneous effects'. On the rare occasion that something choice turns up, the general auction affords the best opportunity of picking up a bargain, as neither the cataloguer nor other bidders present are likely to have specialist knowledge on, or keen interest in, what is mistakenly still regarded as a minor branch of the antiques trade. However, as might be expected, the majority of coins sold in this way are mishandled, being considered of no consequence, or else really are of little value, and they hardly justify the time and expense of anyone looking for good coins to attend such auctions. It is interesting and significant to note that 'rubbish' often fetches better prices in a general auction than it would in one which specialises in coins, because people who buy coins in the former usually have only a superficial interest in them, with little knowledge, and tend to overestimate both condition and the value of large or impressive-looking coins. If there is, therefore, any market for cheap or inferior coins, this is where it is most likely to be, although any profits to be made will not be large in actual terms: £1 for a cupro-nickel 1977 Silver Jubilee crown, paid at such an auction, is more than the London dealers' retail price, but it won't make the seller rich!

Specialist coin auctions, on the other hand, will have both worthwhile coins and also more knowledgeable bidders. Neverthe-less, this is the main source of supply for many dealers and, more frequently than is generally appreciated, an outlet they often use to clear out or test the market on coins which have proved difficult to sell by direct means. Generally, when dealers compete, the margins of profit will be reduced, as most of them will be pretty well in touch with the latest tendencies, knowing for which coins there is currently a strong or a weak demand. Not all dealers, of course, experience the same strength of demand, which varies with the tastes and pockets of their particular clientèle. A Swiss dealer, for example, should be able to outbid an English dealer in London for Swiss coins, and in Zürich the English dealer should be able to outbid the Swiss for English coins. Most dealers know their good customers well enough to judge if they will want to buy and pay well for certain expensive coins, and they will thus be able to bid strongly for any such coins, with a fair likelihood of being able to resell them quickly.

This form of 'natural selection' operates at all auctions. When a £1,000 coin is up for sale, in most instances the price curtails the number of active bidders and their activity. When low-value coins are auctioned, those who bid enthusiastically for better coins are quite likely to have little interest, if any, and leave the field open to a different group of bidders. As a result of such diversification of interests and resources, dealers can peacefully compete in specialist auctions without stepping on each others' toes too much. But where the coins in auction are in universal demand and within the financial reach of many bidders, there is sure to be tough competition and a good price for the seller.

Turning to the specific, clearly the highest prices will normally be paid for coins in the country of their origin, and, if possible, coins should be sold where the interest, and demand, is likely to be greatest; and, conversely, bought where demand and competition is most likely to be weak. A buyer should look abroad for opportunities to buy coins of his own country at low prices.

Apart from this, certain markets have their own peculiar features. Some are more quality-conscious than others, perhaps because the proportion of wealthy to less wealthy collectors in these countries is higher than in others. Ancient Greek and Roman coins of quality are particularly appreciated in Switzerland, while lesser specimens fare better in auction in London. The US market, while always good for the choicest coins of most countries, is insular in that by far the keenest trading there involves American coins. The high volume of trading is reflected in the fine pitch to which the market there is tuned, justifying the weekly publication of an index showing price movements for each type of each denomination of US coin.

To reap full benefit at an auction, the sensible buyer should be flexible. He should not expect to buy coins of a country in which many of the others present are likely to be interested. He should be sufficiently versatile to recognise opportunities in as diverse a field as possible. In any world of cut-throat competition, having merely a slight edge over the opposition produces results which can be repeated time and again, to excellent effect. By noting even an area or auction house in which there is a tendency for certain coins to realise unusually low or high prices, one can buy reasonably or sell profitably. Dealers who travel widely – as many do – are well aware of the advantages obtainable as a result of local and international coin preferences.

Perhaps less widely appreciated is the fact that some coins, even if choice and in the country of their origin, will not realise their full potential at certain auctions, but will at others. When they are looking for particular or unusual coins, collectors contact the larger dealers or go to the largest city, where dealers tend to congregate: the odds on finding the coins are best where the greatest volume of stock is located. In a provincial auction it is therefore less likely that an important coin of an obscure type, of which there are relatively few collectors, will realise a good price than it would at an established large-city auction house, which will probably have a mailing-list extending abroad as well as throughout the country, and thus maximise the small number of potential bidders.

As a rule, higher prices will be realised at auctions which contain a good collection or group of coins of similar type than at those where the coins are of mixed types and equal in quality. Fewer collectors notice or bother to attend an auction in which only an odd one or two coins may interest them; but a host of choice and rare coins generates enthusiasm and draws collectors from far and wide, resulting in keen competition and, often, record prices. When a number of keen and knowledgeable bidders compete, they will be aware of how seldom a particular coin may appear for sale or how unusually choice another may be, and this appreciation of the coin's virtues will be reflected in the strength of their bidding; whereas most or all of them will more easily overlook the same coin if it is slipped in alongside others of lesser consequence or outside their specialised interest. For these reasons, a seller with only one or two coins of an unusual type does best to include them in an auction with others of a similar type, if he can wait.

It is therefore useful to note any tendencies for particular auction houses to achieve high prices for certain types of coin, in order to sell there; or any tendencies in the opposite direction, which will indicate the chance to buy cheaply. By knowing in advance of a sale involving the former, one can include any important coins one has of the appropriate type, and thus take advantage of a seller's market. Contact with auctioneers can be helpful in this respect.

Before buying or selling, it is important to attend an auction

personally and to examine the coins to be sold. This applies in
particular where the auction house holds infrequent coin sales and,
through inexperience, might make mistakes in grading or catalog-
uing. They may also be unable to devote much time to the checking of
each coin in detail, having more lucrative auction material, and they
may have only general reference books on coins. By checking that
they are competent, you can avoid purchases or sales resulting in a
loss due to their errors or omissions. Also, a printed grade by itself will
not indicate the quality of strike, or a particularly pleasing or ugly
patina, which has to be seen to be appreciated, and which will
certainly add to or detract from the value. Even good photographs
may fail to do justice to the finer points of condition, so, if bidding,
examine the coins.

When the auctioneer has a tendency to overgrade, the prices
obtained seem to be low, unless one has actually seen the coins and
realised that they were not as good as stated. Those who bid will have
examined the coins and made their bids according to their own
interpretation of the coins' grades; but the result is that others, who
only read about the coins and the prices they realised, and who did not
examine them, may be misled into believing that bargains are to be
picked up there.

Other auctioneers do the opposite and undergrade, ostensibly to be
sure of satisfying very discriminating postal bidders who will be happy
when they see what they have bought and derive greater confidence
in buying from them, sight unseen. This is, of course, a genuine
benefit to the auctioneer, although postal bidding normally accounts
for only a small proportion of sales at auction. In fact, undergrading
also, and perhaps primarily, serves to encourage potential sellers who,
looking at prices realised in previous sales, will come to the conclusion
that very high prices are consistently achieved there, and will be
encouraged to sell through them. Of course, the VF coin which sells at
a remarkably high £100 would be graded by most people as an EF
coin, and £100 then may be quite a modest price for the coin. Most
pre-sale estimates serve a similar purpose. These tend to be less than
the auctioneer really expects, and after the sale they permit him to
show how successful the sale was, 'beyond expectations'. They do, of
course, serve some purpose as a guide to buyers, and probably help to
encourage bidding by giving the impression that the coins might go
cheaply, whereas a more realistic estimate might deter some potential

bidders, if they thought the real worth of the coins was likely to be fully appreciated.

Only by attending and examining the coins, and having correct judgement and experience in grading, will you be able to decide if there is a bias in either direction and assess correctly whether or not a particular auction house offers a genuine advantage as a buying or selling outlet. Another and an important reason for making one's own judgement on coins in auction is that many auctioneers disclaim any responsibility for errors in description, grading, or even the genuineness of what they state in their catalogue they are offering for sale. The rule is 'caveat emptor' – let the buyer beware. While no reputable auctioneer would hesitate to refund money for a forgery which he had sold as a genuine article, a few might be unwilling to do so, so it is as well to know your auctioneers in addition to your coins!

It is important to remember to allow for charges made and deducted by auctioneers from the 'knock-down' price, especially if you are relying on a narrow profit margin. Their commissions vary roughly between 10 and 15 per cent, plus, in Britain, Value Added Tax. Additionally, there may be charges for insurance and photographs in the catalogue, so, when selling, do not forget to allow for these deductions when estimating how much you can expect to receive.

It might be appropriate here to draw attention to the importance of correct costing, generally. At the time of writing (mid-1982), in Britain any coin or set of coins sold for over £3,000 is subject to Capital Gains Tax of 15 per cent on the profit. All coins which are less than one hundred years old, including gold, are liable for VAT at the standard rate of 15 per cent. Some dealers include the VAT in the price while others add it on, so it is important to know which is the case before buying modern coins. If you are so successful that you decide to make trading in coins your profession, you may have to register with the VAT office, and, instead of Capital Gains Tax, you will be taxed on all profits, but with allowance for expenses.

Remember also that, unless or until you turn professional, you will incur non-deductible expenses, such as travelling, insurance, postal, and advertising. When, finally, you find you have a net profit, compare it with the net rate of interest you might otherwise have received if you had invested your money instead, and if it is not significantly greater, either try to buy and sell coins more efficiently or give it up!

Some writers, at this point, might add that you will perhaps be rewarded by the pleasure or fun you receive from owning, albeit temporarily, beautiful or interesting coins. I would prefer to suggest that you concentrate on the cold, hard business of succeeding, first and foremost. If not, your judgement may easily be impaired by subjectivity, as the 'lure' of wanting a pretty or important coin may distract you from considering whether or not it is a viable economic proposition. It will be a bonus, in an intangible sense, if it does give you pleasure or fun to own or handle coins: it has to be reasonably interesting, at the very least, or else you would put your time and efforts to another use.

Returning to the subject of auctions, most of the coin auctioneers do not charge a 'buyer's premium'; but many general auctioneers do, and, as this naturally affects the price paid to the buyer, by over 10 per cent normally, it is useful to clarify whether or not a premium is applicable.

All the above advice on buying and selling at auction is based on the assumption that free and unfettered market forces apply. In other words, that bidding is made and prices arrived at by straightforward means. Unfortunately, it has been known occasionally for an auctioneer to raise the bidding artificially by 'bouncing bids off the chandelier', or calling up on bids they do not have, usually to bring prices up to or near the limit of a postal or commission bid which they have received. These are bids made by the auctioneer on behalf of a bidder who wishes to remain anonymous or who is not present at the sale. The auctioneer is instructed to bid for the client up to a certain limit, and is on trust to try to buy for as low a price as possible, in so far as other bids permit. The vast majority of auctioneers can be trusted to do this, but there are always exceptions. It is safest to attend auctions personally and bid oneself, opting out if there is any hint of unethical practices.

Another ploy occasionally used at auction, from the other side of the counter, so to speak, is the buyers' 'ring'. This involves a group of bidders who agree beforehand that only one of the group will make bids for a particular item, which several of them may want. This eliminates competition between individuals in the group at the auction, and thus may keep the prices realised artificially low. Afterwards, the benefit gained is calculated and shared out among the parties concerned. Although illegal, this and other methods of unfairly influencing auction results are difficult to detect and therefore to prevent. Happily, they are the exception, but it is best for anyone intending to buy or sell at a particular auction to attend an earlier one and satisfy himself that no such activities go on there, before becoming involved financially. As an additional precaution, the seller of an important coin should place a 'reserve' price – i.e. instruct the auctioneer not to sell – if bidding fails to reach his minimum acceptable figure for it.

Many buyers at specialist auctions are dealers, some of whom are bidding on instructions from collectors, for a small commission. This enables the collector who cannot attend personally to entrust his bids to someone whom he knows and who has no vested interest in raising the price artificially. If a number of collectors give the same dealer their various bids on the same item, the dealer gains more than just a commission from the successful customer: he charges the highest bidding customer an amount in excess of the next highest bid he has, as well as the commission on it, irrespective of the actual amount which he, the dealer, paid at the auction. The seller loses, in that, if the bids were actually made or otherwise lodged with the auctioneer, a higher knock-down price, and one reflecting the true bidding figures, would result. At best, this seems like a legalised version of the 'ring', operating to reduce the knock-down price, with the difference that any and all gains go to the dealer; at worst, the dealer can charge his successful customer anything up to the limit he set, and be able to claim he had other commission bids necessitating this, when he did not.

Advertising

With the drawbacks and pitfalls possible in other methods, many prefer to buy and sell by advertising in a coin magazine. On the surface, this would seem to be the ideal outlet, reaching thousands of collectors and many dealers. There is, certainly, the cost of placing advertisements, which can be substantial; but this may not be prohibitive if the value of the coins sold compensates. The first problem, however, is that they may not be sold. Pricing one's coins sufficiently cheaply to compete with, or undercut, dealers and other advertisers may, after deduction of costs, leave no profit; and pricing up may inhibit sales to the point where the costs of advertising result in a net loss.

Then there is the element of risk. This applies more for potential buyers than sellers, as most advertisers ask for pre-payment of coins ordered, stating they will refund within a certain period if the coins are not satisfactory. Many collectors are loathe to send money for something they have not seen to someone whom they do not know, and this worry undoubtedly acts as a deterrent to many would-be buyers. Trust and confidence that the coins will be genuine, correctly described, and properly graded, are what enable established dealers to sell from the regular sales lists which some of them issue. The unfortunate fact is that the currency of trust has been debased by a few who overgrade absurdly, probably intending to sell to novices who have little idea of grading and who are willing to believe that what a professional dealer states must be correct. An advertiser of this sort will be likely to receive back a substantial proportion of the coins he sends out, but some will remain sold, either to the ignorant or to others who optimistically consider the overgrading to be of minor concern and who, through inertia and the cost involved in returning coins properly covered for insurance, do nothing.

Fortunately, there exist professional bodies whose concern it is to protect and maintain high standards in coin dealing. In Britain, there is the British Numismatic Trade Association,* and those dealers who are members are pledged to maintain those standards.

Coin fairs

The fairly recent development of coin fairs has enabled many small traders and others whose outlets are restricted, to reach a wider public. This must be beneficial, not only for such traders, but also for collectors, as the competition resulting from having numerous sellers of similar goods under one roof helps to keep the price of all except very rare or exceptional coins down to a moderate level.

There is often a good deal of inter-dealer trading during the early part of a fair, as those coins which seem to be cheap are snapped up. As a result, and with so many knowledgeable professionals present, there is very little scope to make a purchase likely to yield the buyer a good early profit.

Perhaps more surprisingly, a fair is not a guarantee of a sellers' market. In spite of the potential competition, so long as dealers can

---

* The address is given on page 90.

buy from the uninformed public or half-informed collectors, they have no need to pay more to people who are aware of and want the correct value of their coins. Nor is there a chance to conduct a 'Dutch auction' with an especially important coin. Most dealers present will be aware of each other's stock of better coins, and also of each other's particular 'wants'. Dealers will not compete for a coin they know to be required by a competitor, unless, of course, they themselves have a customer who will purchase it. Instead, many will delay a decision whether or not to buy until they have shown it to another dealer who really does want it, and thereby obtain an immediate resale, even if the actual profit is not great. If the seller then offers it to the dealer who really will pay well, the latter has no need to do so, knowing that, by declining to offer more, the seller will probably return to the first dealer and accept his price. The coin can then be resold between the dealers, to their mutual gain.

7

Conclusions

The coin market, in common with most human activities, is not exactly predictable, and it may sometimes turn out to be difficult to sell a coin which hitherto 'performed well', and which, from all indications, should be easy to sell. Perhaps demand, while strong, was limited, enabling a few sellers to obtain high prices, and it has been satisfied, as a result. If you find you are stuck with such a coin, consider trying outlets you may have overlooked. Demand can vary quite a lot from one part of the country to another, and from one country to another. In addition, in some areas potential buyers for the coin may have only out-of-date statistics, which will give no hint of the fallen demand which you know, from experience, to be the current position; and they may, as a result, be keen to buy it, as you were.

Wide-awake dealers who themselves have no customer are quick to buy a coin for which they know there will be a demand elsewhere. Statistics are not available, but it is likely that many of the more expensive coins being offered for sale at any given time are bought and sold more frequently between the dealing fraternity than to or from collectors.

If there really is no opportunity to resell a good coin profitably, keep it, if you can afford to, because it will be in demand again, some time, and, as experience shows, good coins which have stagnated for a few years do not simply increase in value when they eventually appreciate – they jump!

It all goes back to having the right coins at the right prices, when selling will be easy. The problem is to find coins for which there is a constant demand, or just desirable coins at low prices; and this is becoming harder. With priced catalogues readily available, most collectors and many non-collectors know, or can easily find out, what coins they have and their approximate value. As a result, opportunities to make a killing by buying valuable coins for next-to-nothing are much less frequent than they once were. Another factor working in favour of the seller is the large number of dealers now active, compared with the few who monopolised the coin scene until 1960 or so. Even if an odd one tries to hoodwink an inexperienced seller, there is no shortage of dealers to approach, and he should be offered a fairly reasonable price by some of the others. It is, clearly, not advisable to accept the first figure offered. With the dramatic increase in active dealers over the last twenty years or so, it follows that the volume of trading in coins has also increased by leaps and bounds, and this, in turn, reflects increases in the number of collectors and investors.

Nor is each coin market as insular and self-contained as in previous years. Dealers have become progressively more active in trading in foreign coins, seeing and taking opportunities where they are to be found; and they travel more, both to buy and to sell, in other countries. International coin fairs attract a large number of foreign buyers and sellers, on both sides of the counter, and, with the travelling and other expenses involved, they must really find it worthwhile.

Both the continually increasing number of active collector/investors and the growing trade in coins between one country and another must act as a form of buffer to coin prices. Where demand for certain coins once may have almost ceased to exist, now it simply recedes, as a consequence. If one economy falters or fails, there will still be collectors and investors to buy coins of that country, abroad. They will have less competition and prices will drop to some extent, but there will at least be a market for the coins.

The conclusion to be drawn is that for most coins, and for those which appeal to collectors everywhere in particular, the element of risk is slight and ever lessening. It would take something approaching a breakdown of the complete economy of the West to wipe out coin values over the board. Nowadays, it is considered something of a minor disaster when a coin fails to appreciate over a period of more than five years. So long as the coin market remains free and unfettered, there is every reason to expect past trends, in good times and bad, to continue, and when one can plan, as opposed to guess, confidence in the way one invests is bound to grow also. In all trade, planners make predictions based on observation and experience. Large enterprises spend much money in researching to be able to plan for future buying trends, and, while coins are not in the same category as foodstuffs or hardware, a similarly reasoned and methodical approach will come up with a fair percentage of right answers just the same.

The ebb and flow of prices is not unlike that of tidal movements, with successive waves adding to or removing from the overall level of the water, and with the interaction of seas, rivers and streams helping to offset any dramatic change in localised input or output. Profits can be made by correct anticipation, or early detection, of a strengthening demand for particular coins, and by buying from sources where that demand has not yet become apparent, or, equally, by selling where it has. Pre-knowledge was once the mysterious privilege of a few, when dealers simply locked away in bank vaults certain choice coins they had bought, in order that, once supplies had dried up, they could bring them out and offer them for sale at the rather higher prices brought about by the then strong and protracted demand for such coins.

Literature informing on all aspects of coins is much more plentiful than ever before, and information regarding the availability or otherwise of particular types of coin plays a significant part in profitable buying and selling. We have considered how the state of a country's economy may affect the price of its coins, and forecasts for the former can be used as a guide to deciding whether to buy or sell the coins of that country. In a similar way, pre-knowledge of an important specialist sale is useful, as the sale can be expected to give an impetus to demand, and most prices – of the choicest coins in particular – will probably be higher after it than they were before. The person who has a little more knowledge or information will always have an advantage.

The well-publicised Duke of Hamilton collection of British milled coins was auctioned in early 1979, and it gave a strong fillip to the price of most coins of this type. Notable exceptions were poorer and even average specimens of all but the important rarities. Over a year later, in a less 'bullish' atmosphere, many of the less important coins from that sale were being re-auctioned and realising less than they did at the Hamilton sale. Perhaps the generally high prices paid for EF and better coins at the specialist sale influenced bidders to overbid for the lower-value coins, and the prices these made were subsequently shown not to reflect true demand. In other words, they were bought by dealers or investors who wrongly anticipated that, after and as a result of the sale, collectors of lower-grade specimens would be willing to accept a general price increase. They were not. The likely answer is that the deepening economic recession was hitting the pockets of those collectors who might otherwise have bought the average specimens, whereas wealthy collectors and those with money to invest want quality only. Even in hard times, the money can always be produced by someone when really outstanding coins are on the market.

Since the sale, top-quality coins in general and crowns in particular continued to increase in value at a high rate. This was shown most markedly by the example of the 1736 crown. The Hamilton specimen, 'almost EF', realised £700, while fifteen months later, another of this date, 'about EF' but with some weak letters and a small flaw, tripled this in another auction by the same company, fetching £2,100.

Another way in which particular coin prices can be stimulated is by the publication of a good specialised book. This has the effects both of drawing attention to a particular series of coins and also of making it more understandable and thus easier to enjoy and collect. Prior to the publication in 1958 of *Copper, Tin and Bronze Coins in the British Museum, 1558–1958*, by C.W. Peck, a book which is rightly considered a classic work, there was no catalogue adequately covering the many types of these coins. Those books which existed failed to set them out in a logical or coherent format, and significant omissions were subsequently seen to be almost as plentiful as those types which were included. With the publication of Peck's catalogue, a substantial up-swing in demand for, and the price of, copper and bronze coins occurred as a direct result, simply because it was now possible and simple to identify and form a systematic collection of them.

Will past trends continue? For many, it is hard to conceive that today's 'high' prices will increase to the extent by which they have in the past fifteen years or so; but it was even harder, fifteen years ago, to foresee the level prices are at today. It is more relevant to ask why they should not continue than why they should. Given the same strength of demand, it would appear that there should be no alternative. It may even be more reasonable now than ever before to expect continuing price rises, as everyone is inured to them through the advent and acceptance of a high inflation rate as normal.

While this may well be true as a general rule, there will, clearly, continue to be 'stickers' – bad investments – where price increases, if any, drag behind the average. There will, with equal certainty, be 'leaders' – coins underpriced in the light of demand or supply, and not yet appreciated as such. These are where future high profits are going to be found.

Almost everyone who becomes involved with old coins finds them interesting, fun, or exciting, depending on his approach to them. For them to be financially rewarding, however, which is your prime concern, you must subordinate all considerations other than the following:

(1) Is it available at a good price?
(2) Is there a good demand for it?

If it also gives you pleasure to own for a while, that should be considered a bonus; but hard facts and cool, objective judgement are a necessity if you intend to put out a lot of money on coins, because those which are not satisfactory as investments far outnumber those which are.

You are bound to make mistakes: the most experienced dealers do quite often, as witnessed by the fact that they have to hang on to some coins for a long time, and their not infrequent use of auctions as a selling medium. Perhaps the flaw on a coin puts people off more than you thought it would when you bought it; or perhaps you bought a popular coin just when it had 'peaked' and the market for it has since stagnated. If possible, to cover such contingencies, it is clearly best to pay less than you believe it to be worth to you. A dealer needs to maintain a stock of coins he can sell and sometimes will have to take a gamble in buying a coin which may just be profitable or may be a little pricey. Those who do not require a regular income or cash flow can afford to be more choosey. There may be periods when good opportunities to buy well simply do not occur – and, when in doubt, do not buy. There is a steady flow of coins on to the market, and some are bound to be both in demand and available cheaply. When you do make the mistake of overpaying, you will just either have to accept a loss, if you have to maintain a cash flow, or hold on to the coin until its price rises, if you can afford to. When it happens too often, give up!

Hopefully, there will also be occasions when you will have unknowingly paid cheaply for a coin. Perhaps you will *never* know, if you simply added on what you believed to be a reasonable profit and sold the coin, too cheaply. No one is likely to tell you if you are doing this – at least, not until they have bought it! If you are, by putting it into auction, you will not miss out in this way, as the bidding will progress beyond your mistaken expectations.

Research thoroughly and know what you are buying. Information on latest prices being paid, on which rare varieties to look out for, and any relevant articles, should be sought. Books read and magazines subscribed to will often repay their cost, at some time or another. An article reporting a recently discovered hoard of coins all of a certain type may help to prevent you overpaying for what all sale lists and catalogues hitherto refer to as a high-priced rarity. The article may be of no interest to you when you first glance at it, but it is most useful to have a library with information on all branches of numismatics for just such an occasion.

The best source of information is, in spite of various provisos and qualifications, auction catalogues with prices realised. These are the equivalent of field study in science. A collection of them, over a period, should be pretty comprehensive, and give, or help to assess, current values more accurately than any other source.

In the same way as no book or article can possibly tell you how to win the football pools, so there is no fool-proof, guaranteed way to make a fortune in coins; and even if there were such a way, anyone who knew of it would hardly divulge such valuable information to others.

What you have read here is a frank, candid and objective view of the best method to tackle coin investment. It can only be a guide in the right direction, as the art of prediction has not yet been perfected. Used as such, it should prove invaluable so long as coins remain the healthy and profitable investment they have shown themselves to be.

Useful addresses

The following addresses and telephone numbers may be useful:

The International Bureau for the Suppression of Counterfeit Coins (IBSCC), London W1, 01-486 5178

The British Museum, London WC1B 3DG, 01-636-1555 (ext. 271)

The Royal Mint Museum, Llantrisant, Pontyclun, Mid Glamorgan, CF7 8YT, 0443-222111

Coin Monthly, Sovereign House, Brentwood, Essex, CM14 4SE, 0277-219876

American Numismatic Association, PO Box 2366, Colorado Springs, Co 80901, USA (303) 473-9142

British Numismatic Trade Association, Mrs C. Deane (secretary), PO Box 52c, Esher, Surrey, KT10 8PW, 0372-62568

Some well-established London coin dealers:

B.A. Seaby, Ltd, Audley House, 11 Margaret Street, London W1N 8AT, 01-580-3677

Spink & Son, Ltd, 5–7 King Street, St James's, London SW1Y 6QR, 01-930-7888

A.H. Baldwin & Co., Ltd, 11 Adelphi Terrace, London WC2N 6BJ, 01-839-1310

Some well-established coin auctioneers:

Glendining & Co., 7 Blenheim Street, New Bond Street, London W1Y 9LD, 01-493-2445

Christie's, 8 King Street, St James's, London SW1Y 6QT, 01-839-9060

Sotheby's, 34–35 New Bond Street, London W1A 2AA, 01-493-8080

Index